We see them, players like Jeremy Affeldt, on TV. They are stars because they are Major Leaguers—the dream I had as a boy and the dream my son had. But we wonder what their life—their inner life, their family life—is really like. Too often we hear of corruption and carousing and infidelity. We are tempted to be cynical. But *To Stir a Movement* tells the inner life of a young man revolutionized by Jesus Christ. Jeremy Affeldt's life is the story that happens when grace takes root and turns a selfish young man into a Major Leaguer whose life off the field matters more than what we will ever see on the field. I thank God for Jeremy.

Scot McKnight
Professor of New Testament
Northern Seminary

If you like baseball, or if you are interested in faith, or if you have a social conscience and would like the world to be a better place, or if you would like to be inspired, or if you love a riveting story of challenge and resilience, you gotta read this book. Otherwise, check your pulse. This is not just a book about the faith of an athlete; it's a book about changing the world.

John Ortberg
Pastor, Menolo Park (California) Presbyterian Church
Author, *The Me I Want to Be* and *Who Is This Man?*

Jeremy Affeldt proves time and time again that he is a most unique professional athlete. He plays the game on another level—not just for himself but for a world of the orphan, the widow, the exploited. He does not make lofty endorsements that might make himself look good in the media. Instead, he takes principled action so that he can stand with integrity behind his words. I have seen Jeremy connect with kids in a rescue village in northern Thailand and in the inner city of Los Angeles, so I can testify to the extraordinary lengths he will go to see justice roll in our broken world. Read this book and be inspired to turn the thing you most love to do into a vehicle for change and hope.

David Batstone
Co-founder and President of Not For Sale

Jeremy Affeldt may be a two-time World Series champion and one of the greatest left-handed relievers in major league baseball, but that is just the tip of the iceberg as to the man that he is. As you will read in this book, Jeremy is not defined by baseball. He is defined and validated as a child and follower of the most high God. My hope is that this book will help define and validate you.

Mike Sweeney
Five-Time American League All Star
Sixteen seasons Major League Baseball

TO STIR A MOVEMENT

TO STIR A MOVEMENT

LIFE, JUSTICE, AND MAJOR LEAGUE BASEBALL

JEREMY AFFELDT

BEACON HILL PRESS
OF KANSAS CITY

These are the experiences as I saw them.

Solus Christus

To my parents, who gave me opportunities
to dream as they launched me on my journey
through life, and
to my beautiful wife, Larisa, who joined me
on this journey and has loved me and
encouraged me all along the way.

Library of Congress Cataloging-in-Publication Data

Affeldt, Jeremy, 1979-
  To stir a movement : life, justice, and Major League Baseball / Jeremy Affeldt.
    pages cm
  ISBN 978-0-8341-3051-7
  1. Affeldt, Jeremy, 1979- 2. Baseball players—United States—
Biography. 3. Baseball players—United States—Biography. 4. Christian athletes—United States—Biography. 5. Christian athletes—Religious life. I. Title.
  GV865.A266A3 2013
  796.357092—dc23
  [B]
                                                          2012046543

10 9 8 7 6 5 4 3 2 1

CONTENTS

1   Thailand   10

2   Dad   16

3   Teenage Angst   30

4   Redeemed   42

5   Larisa   52

6   Moving On Up   68

7   A Royal Pain: Part 1   82

8   A Royal Pain: Part 2   94

9   Rocky Mountain Highs   108

10 Cincinnati Lows   120

11 Striking Out Injustice   132

12 World Series #2   142

13 Generation Alive   160

14 Blessed Beyond Imagination   172

Afterword   189

Extra Innings: One Final Story   191

ONE

Suddenly, out of nowhere a man grabbed my arm and began pulling me into the building. I tried to resist as he insisted there was something inside he wanted me to see. The man didn't see my dad— he just saw me, a tanned towhead.

SIXTY FEET. Only sixty feet.

The memory is a blur really. There were people scurrying around, intensely heading somewhere along with the commotion of motorcycle carts and vendors and lots of bronze and gold Buddha statues everywhere. I was only about ten years old and on vacation with my family in Thailand. My dad is a career military man in the United States Air Force, a bombardier. When I was in the second grade he was transferred to Guam, so my family traveled all over Asia when I was a kid.

True to my adventurous self, I had run ahead of my dad. I wasn't too far ahead, about the distance from the pitcher's mound to home plate. It must have appeared that I was wandering alone in the bustling city as I passed what I later found out was a strip club, a sex shop catering mostly to Westerners who came to Thailand to act out their perversions. Suddenly, out of nowhere a man grabbed my arm and began pulling me into the building. I tried to resist as he insisted there was something inside he wanted me to see. The man didn't see my dad—he just saw me, a tanned towhead.

My dad quickly came to my rescue. Fortunately, his eyes had been fixed on me as I ventured ahead. He separated me from the stranger and pushed the man away with what must have been a superhuman surge of adrenaline. I was surprised by the way my dad was yelling at him, creating quite a ruckus—kind of like a pro wrestler threatening his opponent. Except this wasn't an act. At the time, I thought dad was overreacting to the idea of my talking to strangers. Almost as soon as it started, it was over. And I didn't think anything more about that incident until twenty years later.

A couple of weeks after signing with the San Francisco Giants, my whole world changed. I had just seen a headline about human trafficking in the newspaper. My friend Mike was at my house, and I asked him what he knew about trafficking.

I really didn't think it was that big of an issue. I was completely oblivious. Mike said that I should get in touch with Dave Batstone and learn more about his group, Not for Sale.

So I googled it.

Not for Sale is an organization that educates, equips, and mobilizes activists to "deploy innovative solutions to re-abolish slavery in their own backyards and across the globe."

On the Not for Sale web site I started reading about modern-day slavery and the horrors of human trafficking. Suddenly as I was reading these stories, my wife, Larisa, exclaimed, "Dave Batstone is in Half Moon Bay!" I couldn't believe it. When she said he was a professor at the University of San Francisco, I knew I had to get in touch with him.

I searched for an e-mail address online and sent him a message, although I didn't think it was conceivable that it would reach him. In the message I told him who I was, a pitcher for the San Francisco Giants, and that I was very interested in his organization and would like to learn more about what Not for Sale was doing.

Dave Batstone is a fan of the Giants. When he first read the message, he was convinced that someone from within his organization was pranking him. But when no one would admit to sending him the e-mail, he replied to me within an hour.

Larisa and I were going to San Francisco for FanFest, so we were able to arrange a dinner with Dave and his wife. His passion was contagious. The more we talked, the more I felt compelled to join him in Not for Sale's mission.

Did you know that sixty percent of men who fly into Thailand are there on sex tourism trips? They have intentionally purchased a package so they can have illegal sex with a young girl, a child—a kid—and they pay top dollar for it. Girls who should be playing with dolls and coloring books are forced to have sex with a dozen men or more *every day*. The slavery industry as a whole, from child soldiers and children picking cocoa beans to bonded laborers and sweatshop workers and sex slaves, generates more than thirty-two billion dollars every year.

Worldwide, more than thirty million people are trapped in lives bound by slavery.

The odds are good that there's a slave near you. Yes, even right in the USA.

And then it clicked.

I remember looking at Larisa and saying, "Honey, I think I was going to be turned into a slave." I was just a kid, and it was obvious that I was white, even though I was pretty tan. I spent every day outside playing baseball, and the sun had bleached my hair blonde. People would pay good money to have sex with a blonde boy.

What would have happened if my dad had been looking the other way? But he wasn't, and my dad saved me.

Today dads in Thailand who are desperate to survive are selling off their kids as sex slaves. Some have been promised that their child will receive an education and employment in another country. Some simply cannot find any alternative means to make ends meet.

Can you imagine how that child feels?

Children don't have any control over the situation. They are helpless and hopeless. And they are face to face with evil incarnate, a hellacious and disgusting scenario that will haunt them for the rest of their lives.

After visiting with Dave, I knew I had to do something. I had to get involved. To remain uninvolved wasn't even an option. I pledged one hundred dollars for every strikeout for the remainder of the season. The money helped build a hospital in Thailand for girls rescued from sex slavery.

• • •

It took twenty years for God to prepare my heart and to break me and draw me close to His mission in the world, to cause me to want to live out my faith in such a way that the love and servant leadership of Jesus would be transparent in everything I did.

In the movie *The Chronicles of Narnia: Voyage of the Dawn Treader*, the valiant mouse Reepicheep consoles Eustace, the boy-turned-dragon, with these words:

> You know, extraordinary things only happen to extraordinary people. Maybe it's a sign that you've got an extraordinary destiny. Something greater than you could have imagined.

My extraordinary, near-impossible journey to the major leagues, and to hear God's call on my life, started with Dad.

TWO

GUAM WAS A GREAT VENUE FOR TWO GUYS
WHO LOVED TO BE OUTSIDE AND TO SPEND
TIME TOGETHER. I LOVED BEING WITH MY DAD.
HE TAUGHT ME A LOT ABOUT WHAT IT MEANT
TO BE A MAN, A LEADER, AND A LOVER OF LIFE.

I WAS STANDING in center field, warming up at the Oakland (California) Coliseum. I turned my head and stared at the seats where Dad and I had once talked about my professional baseball aspirations. Picking up my cell phone, I gave Dad a call.

"Dad, you'll never guess where I am."

"Oh, I know—you're in Oakland."

"Dad, I'm standing in center field looking at the exact chairs where we were when I said I'd be pitching here one day. And tonight I'll be pitching here, in Oakland."

There was silence on the other end. I could tell that I had caught him off-guard, unprepared for the weight of the conversation. He was choked up. He congratulated me and quickly got off the phone. I knew he was proud of me.

• • •

My parents married shortly after their high school graduation. They met in high school, and my dad was saved at a Billy Graham crusade. Church was always important to both of them. Mom's family has a strong conservative Christian heritage, and Dad comes from a long line of Lutheran pastors. He even inherited a family German Bible dated 1612, which I now have in the prayer room in my home. Dad has always been a strong communicator, and some in his family thought he would be the next pastor in the family.

Shortly after they were married, Dad enlisted with the Air Force, which I'm certain broke some hearts in his family. When my parents married, they had a decision to make regarding their faith—*what church would they attend?* However, in military life more often than not the decision is made for you. You go where you *can* go.

Going to church was a core value of our family. My first memory of church is the church in Guam that we attended as a family. Back then, even though we went every Sunday, I really didn't have a clue as to what church was all about.

Dad was the radar navigator for B-52 airplanes, which meant I had to get used to moving. I was born in Chandler, Arizona, two years after my sister was born. Within a few months we moved. Dad moved the family to Duluth, Minnesota, followed by Sacramento, California, and Spokane, Washington. I was in second grade when we moved to Guam. It was in Guam that I recollect my earliest memories.

Guam is a small island in the western Pacific Ocean. It is only thirty miles long and ten miles wide. Dad was stationed there in the early eighties—during the height of the Cold War. I had some wonderful experiences in Guam, but I also developed some huge fears.

One day I was swimming in the ocean at the beach located on the Air Force base. I remember how much fun I was having in the water when I heard the sirens going off. I looked back to the shore and Dad was waving his hands, motioning me to come back to shore. I thought he was just waving at me, so I waved back. The next thing I knew, a lifeguard came out to get me, lifting me up on a surfboard. He told me not to look back and started swimming hard for the shore. Of course I did what every curious kid does—I turned around and looked back. There was a large hammerhead shark that had flipped over the reef and was on its way toward us. From my childlike perspective, I had barely escaped being eaten alive by a hungry shark. Fear paralyzed me, and I did not ever want to go back into the ocean.

But Dad had different thoughts. Shortly after that close encounter with a hungry shark, my dad decided I needed to get back in the water. There were two beaches near the base. The first was the family beach, where everyone went to play and have a good time. But Dad didn't take me to the family beach. He chose the more adventurous beach. There weren't many families at the second beach. Instead, there were a lot of surfers, because this was the beach with lots of action—where the currents pulled and the waves rolled.

My sister and I jumped into the water, and she was immediately sucked out to the ocean by a rip tide. Dad started running across a coconut field toward her. Thankfully, a surfer rescued her. While all that distraction was happening, I got pulled under by an undertow.

With all my strength I fought to get back to the surface. I panicked and tried to outswim the undertow, but I wasn't strong enough to escape the merciless ocean. Thankfully, another surfer came by and pulled me out of the water by the hair on my head. And that sealed the deal—no more oceans for me. The ocean is not forgiving. It didn't care that I was only a child, and I felt completely helpless and defeated.

Fast-forward two decades from my ocean experiences. I was on vacation with my wife in Maui, and she wanted to go scuba diving. I encouraged her, "Go ahead. You enjoy scuba diving; I'll enjoy the pool and the sand on the beach and watch." She continued to beg me, so being the brave man that I've become—we compromised. We would go snorkeling instead. *Now that's something I can handle*, I thought. *I only have to skim the surface near the beach in calm waters. No problem.*

My wife's parents were with us, as was my sister-in-law and her husband. We saw some beautiful tropical fish, and we were all enjoying ourselves and having a great time. Some tortoises were in the area, so we decided to swim near them to get a closer view. All of a sudden, my wife started screaming. Spontaneously and without a second thought, I turned around and immediately started swimming as hard as I could toward the shore and away from my wife. *Every man for himself! Could be a shark. I'm outta here.* After a few seconds of hard swimming, I turned around, hoping my wife had escaped the jaws of the shark and was headed to safety with me. Instead, she was standing in the shallow water looking at me with her hands in the air. "What are you doing?"

I casually swam back to her and said, "You were screaming—I thought there could be sharks."

"It was a tortoise," she said. "I just looked up, and his face was right in front of mine. He just scared me a little bit."

To this day she won't let me forget that. I had abandoned my wife because I was afraid I might be eaten alive by sharks. I would like to think that I will always be there for my wife, regardless of the scenario. But if there is the slightest possibility of sharks being involved? Let's just say that everybody's afraid of something.

• • •

I also had some great experiences while we were in Guam. Dad and I would go walking through the jungle and swing on a rope into a freshwater hole and swim around. (There were no sharks.) Dad also took me to Talofofo Falls, and we jumped off the cliffs into the water. Guam was a great venue for two guys who loved to be outside and to spend time together. I loved being with my dad. He taught me a lot about what it meant to be a man, a leader, and a lover of life.

• • •

When I was in fifth grade I bade farewell to Guam. Dad was transferred to Merced, California, where he worked as an instructor at the Air Force base there— teaching, training, and writing curriculum for young aviators. Operation Desert Storm started during this time, and Dad really wanted to go, but Mom wanted him to stay home with me and my sister. I remember how happy I was that he didn't go.

As a military kid, I learned to make friends quickly. I also learned not to take it too hard when it's time to move. I've always been sociable, because I've had to be. All this helped prepare me for life in the major leagues. To this day, I can still see the faces of friends from all the places I've lived, but I struggle to remember their names. That's one of the tough parts of life in the military—the difficulty in developing deep, intentional, lifelong friends.

• • •

As long as I can remember, I've loved playing baseball. I played every day when we were in Guam. My skin was tanned, the sun bleached my hair blonde, and the red clay permanently stained my clothes and uniform. In Guam I started learning how to pitch. I've always thrown the ball hard, and I loved the thrill of throwing it right past a swinging batter.

When we moved from Guam to California, I was in a league in which you pitched to your own teammates.

The idea was that you would throw it easy enough for your teammate to hit the ball. I was completely and utterly frustrated by the concept. It wasn't what I was used to, coming from Guam. *Why would I want to pitch against my own team? Why can't I pitch against the other team?* Finally, my coach came out to me and said, "You've got to let them hit it. Throw it easier."

My dad approached the coach and said, "He's not used to playing like that. He's used to striking out his opponents." So they didn't let me pitch anymore that year.

While I was growing up there wasn't the mentality that there is today to train your kid to be a superstar from birth. I went to only one sports camp—as a seventh grader—sponsored by the local junior college. It cost only twenty bucks. I played whatever sport I wanted—baseball, soccer, basketball. I didn't think about "specializing" in a sport. I didn't play football, because Mom thought I might break in half. I was pretty much a toothpick.

Too many parents today try to live vicariously through their children, pushing them to succeed and choose only one sport to play. Then they send them to expensive, intense camps all over the country. Dad didn't do that with me. He and Mom just watched me play.

When I was in seventh grade, Dad took me to an Oakland Athletics' game at Oakland Coliseum. We arrived early and watched batting practice. I was in awe of the athletes. I was absolutely petrified by the thought of approaching them. I didn't have the courage to ask for a ball or an autograph. Unfortunately, many kids today constantly scream at players who are on the field, "Gimme, gimme, gimme," and then they cuss at you when you don't respond. Dad did not raise me like that.

On that day in Oakland, Dave Stewart, one of my pitching heroes, was on the mound. Mark McGuire, another of my heroes, hit two home runs in the game. As we were watching the game, I looked at Dad and said, "I'm going to play here one day."

Dad looked at me and replied, "You should. Go for it. I think that would be great."

I don't think Dad thought I really had a chance of playing in the major leagues, but it was my dream, and he wasn't going to kill it. Dad let me dream as big as I could dare to imagine, and he and Mom stood behind me all the way. They were always my best fans.

• • •

When I was only twelve years old, I decided, for some reason, that I wanted to referee some of the local soccer games. Dad let me do it. He came to the games and watched me as I ran up and down the field chasing mobs of five-year-olds. Parents from both sidelines screamed and yelled at me, and he let them do it. "You're a referee," he said. "It comes with the territory." He thought it was good for me to develop thick skin. He's a military man, you know, and there's not too much soft about him.

But a father can take only so much. There have been times during my major league career when fans in the stands boo and yell at me. My dad politely lets them know—"Be careful—that's my son you're talking about."

Dad has always been in my corner, but if I had a bad attitude or displayed bad character on the field, he wouldn't let me play. I learned this lesson quickly.

His faithful, consistent presence was a gift. We played catch or shot baskets together. One time I threw the ball over his head and right through one of the windows on our house. I remember his saying, "Well, I guess we'll have to fix that." He didn't get angry and yell. He knew I didn't do it intentionally. He was with me through everything. He was my true coach.

I learned many things from Dad over the years. One of the most important life lessons he drilled into me is to never, ever quit.

I first experienced failure playing in Lansing, Michigan, my second year in the minor leagues when I was eighteen. It was 1998, and I had just graduated from high school and was carrying an ERA (earned run average) over nine. I was awful. Everyone I pitched against was better than me; they were older than me, and they had played *college* ball. Every time I threw a pitch, I gave up hits and runs and more hits and more runs. Nothing was going my way. I started thinking that I hated baseball.

Sitting in my host family's home, I called Dad and told him what I was thinking. *I'm uncomfortable here. I'm uncomfortable on the field. Nothing feels right. I don't want to do this anymore. I want to come home. I don't want to play anymore.*

Dad asked, "Jeremy, is the reason you don't want to play anymore because you're failing right now, or is it because you think you're not good enough?"

"Well, both, obviously."

"No," Dad replied. "You're failing. Let me tell you a story. One time I was flying a bomb run over a tiny island target off the coast of Guam; it was a live drop. I missed my target. When you miss your target from thirty thousand feet in the air, you don't miss your target by just a few feet. I missed by miles. I almost killed a bunch of fisherman. The bomb blew up in the locals' fishing grounds. As soon as we landed back in Guam, my superiors chewed me out. I was placed on restricted flying status. I was in big trouble. I had made a huge mistake. But I learned from that mistake.

"We all fail. We all make mistakes. You're only eighteen years old, and you're trying to learn how to play ball with men. You're not in high school anymore, Jeremy. You were good in high school because no one else was better than you. But now there are lots of people better than you, and that's okay. You need to fail, but learn from your failures and become better.

"And you can't quit. You can't quit because of a bump in the road. You'll know when it's time to quit, because they won't give you a job."

Dad helped me learn what perseverance really means and how one goes about learning from failure. You're never a failure if you can learn from it.

Too many kids aren't given enough opportunities to fail today. We coddle and pamper and overprotect our kids, trying to help them live the best lives possible. And when they have a chance to fail, a true opportunity to learn how to persevere and succeed, we steal that from them by being overprotective.

In baseball, the best hitters fail seven out of ten times, and we call that a Hall of Fame career. I've been through the trenches in baseball, and I've wanted to quit numerous times. But because I persevered, because I pushed through the failures, I've also been fortunate enough to experience the best of the game. At the time of this writing I've been to the World Series three times, losing with the Colorado Rockies and winning twice with the Giants.

God does not hand us success on a plate. God gifts us and then promises that even though there will be hard times, He will not abandon us. As we learn to lean into our gifts, as we explore and learn how God created us, we can succeed. Success is not necessarily a million bucks or an easy life. Success is doing what God wants you to do with the gifts He has given you.

I thank God for my dad and the way he helped shape me into the man I am today. Dad and Mom, Larisa, and my boys were all there in Texas when we won the World Series. They all came onto the field, and I remember hugging my dad and getting a picture of three generations of Affeldt boys—Dad, me, Walker, and Logan.

In the past couple of years Dad has battled through and beaten cancer, but it took its toll on him. He was depressed and discouraged, and I knew I had to do something.

Motorcycles have always caught Dad's attention. When he was a kid, he rode dirt bikes with his brothers. He had already bought himself a motorcycle he could afford, and he rode it everywhere. He often wanted Mom to ride with him, but it wasn't a very comfortable cycle for her to ride along on.

Larisa and I talked about the situation, and we decided to get Dad a Harley. I went to the shop, and the salesman helped me find a Harley cruiser. He showed me a one-year-old bike with low miles and in great shape. I called Mom and had her come sit on it. She liked it. I told her I wanted to buy it for Dad.

That year we had a Harley Christmas. I bought him boots and a jacket and then told him there was something in the garage that I didn't have time to wrap. We walked out to the garage, and I pointed to a huge tarp covering the motorcycle. He said, "Jeremy, what's this?"

Dad pulled the tarp off of the Harley, and the tears started flowing instantaneously. He hugged me and Larisa. Joy filled my heart seeing my dad's dream come true.

As I was growing up, Dad sacrificed a lot for me. And now I was able to honor and bless him. It felt really good. It was something he couldn't and wouldn't do for himself. I knew this was something he had always wanted, and now I was able to help him achieve one of his dreams. Dad and Mom now go on cruises almost every weekend, seeking adventure and living life.

Looking back, I can see how God has led me, prepared me, and shaped me. I've always envisioned myself as a leader. In order for one to be a leader, there is no better teacher than struggle and pain.

We moved to Spokane right before I started high school. And life got crazy.

THREE

THE WALL I HAD BUILT AROUND MYSELF WAS
TEN MILES HIGH AND FIVE MILES THICK, AND
I WAS FILLING IT WITH BITTERNESS, ANGER,
AND RAGE. IT GOT TO THE POINT WHERE
I REALLY DIDN'T CARE WHAT OTHER
PEOPLE THOUGHT ABOUT ME.

DAD made a career of the military. He served in the Air Force twenty years and retired when I was in high school. His final tour of duty took him to Panama, tracking drug runners. He was gone for an entire year.

Unfortunately, the year he was gone was my freshman year in high school.

In 1993 my parents bought fifteen acres of land in Medical Lake, Washington, just outside of Spokane. They had dreamed of building their own home, and that dream was becoming a reality. The summer after I finished junior high school in Merced, California, we—my mom, sister, and I—moved to Medical Lake and lived in a tent camper while the house was being built. Dad was gone almost the entire year. And that was just the beginning of my horrible introduction to high school.

One day that summer after we had moved, my grandfather took me fishing. We were having a good time, and I decided to change lures. I left the tackle box back in the truck not too far away. I laid down my pole on the dock, the line in the water and a bobber floating on the surface, and started walking up a gentle slope toward the truck. Then, like a scene straight out of the cartoons, a fish snagged my line and pulled my pole into the water. *No way did that just happen,* I thought.

I sprinted back down the hill, accidentally kicked a stump and literally flew toward the dock. When I landed, my head hit the dock, and a nail ripped my lip completely off my face. Blood was pouring out of my face. My grandfather and I both thought my nose was broken. "Let's get you to your mom," he said.

We went back to the tent camper. I walked in and said, "Mom, I think I broke my nose." She told me to move my hand and let her see. As soon as I moved my hand, she dry-heaved. *That's not a broken nose.* She rushed me into the car, and we sped toward the Air Force base and went straight to the hospital.

As we were walking into the hospital, a doctor passed us and looked at me on his way out of the hospital. Immediately, he stopped and addressed my mom. "Ma'am, you guys are coming with me." He took us straight into a room, past all the people waiting in the emergency room. We didn't even really check in. In the room he applied a topical anesthesia and then stuck a needle straight into the open wound on my lip. In case you didn't know, lips have numerous nerve endings and are extremely sensitive.

The pain was excruciating. I was holding Mom's hand for comfort and squeezed so hard I bent the wedding ring around her finger. She didn't flinch. She just encouraged me to keep looking at her, to keep squeezing. She never grimaced, and she never took her eyes off me. My mom is *strong*.

The doctor then took the time to reattach my lip, being intentional and careful about attaching it evenly. The doctor who performed the surgery was one of the best traveling doctors in the military. He was responsible for training others how to sew up wounds. He took the job because he was afraid that if someone else had performed the surgery, I would have a deformed lip or a nasty scar. I was left with a small scar that I have to this day, but it surely seemed like the end of the world in my mid-adolescent phase of life.

Just before the start of school, my classmates were throwing a party, and Mom heard about it. She thought it would be a great idea for me to go to the party and make some new friends. I felt pretty good about going to the party and started introducing myself to others. *Everyone* I talked to stared straight at the new, bright red scar on my face. I was miserable. *Welcome to high school.*

High school is not easy for anyone. In fact, for many it's excruciatingly cruel. High school is an educational institution full of students with raging hormones, attitudes, and questions. Adolescents are struggling with issues of identity and acceptance, trying to learn who they are and find their places in this world. They are definitely not children, yet certainly not adults either. And adults who have forgotten what it's like to be a teenager place them together in one building for eight hours a day, expecting them to sit still, to listen, and to soak up information like a sponge. In high school there are boys bigger than mountains and boys who haven't started growing at all competing for the attention of the same girl. It's in high school where we quickly learn that life is not fair, and sometimes we just do what we can to survive until the next class.

I started high school with Dad out of the country, Mom making all the contracting decisions on the new house, and living in a tent camper. I started high school in a new city, a new state, and I knew no one. Plus, with this "thing" on my face, I knew that I wouldn't be going on any dates in the foreseeable future. *Just great.*

My new school had a huge reputation as a basketball school—state champions. There was a strong basketball program that started even before students were in junior high. The coaches were pretty locked in on everyone's strengths and each player's role on the team. There was no place for a new kid.

I loved to play basketball and was simply trying my best to fit in, to find a place in this new school. I figured the best way to learn the system was to play with the guys who knew the program. So one day as I was playing ball, trying to learn, trying to find my place, one of the guys punched me in the stomach. Out of nowhere, my sister came flying onto the court and shoved the guy onto the ground. Not cool.

Great. Now my sister is fighting my fights. Nothing could be more humiliating than having my older sister sticking up for me and trying to protect me.

Basketball season finally started, and I made the junior varsity team. *Finally*, I thought, *a chance to prove myself.* It's very hard to prove yourself, however, from the bench. As a freshman, I clocked a whopping thirty-two seconds of playing time. Again, my parents wouldn't let me just quit the team. I knew if I had bad grades I couldn't play. But if I had bad grades I wouldn't be allowed to play baseball either, and I knew I was good at baseball. So Mom went and talked to the coach. "Can't you see that my son is struggling? Don't you understand that he's just trying to fit in? This is junior varsity basketball —why can't you play him?"

Now Mom *is fighting my battles. Can things get any worse?*

As a matter of fact, yes, things *could* get worse.

At school, my friends were those who played baseball and soccer. Cliques ruled the school. The basketball team didn't like the baseball or soccer players. I was caught between two groups. My basketball teammates hated me, and my friends couldn't understand why I didn't just quit. Frustration and rage welled up inside of me, and I was a bundle of raw nerves just waiting to explode. Even when Dad called home, I was so mad that I refused to talk to him.

The pain of not playing motivated me to improve. After the season ended, I would come home from school and shoot baskets—even when there was snow on the ground. *Just watch. I'm gonna get so good you'll* have *to play me. I'm not going to allow this to stop me.*

With early spring came baseball season and the chance to finally prove myself; the chance to find my place. I made the varsity team as a freshman and became the winning pitcher that led our team into the state championship playoffs for the first time in the history of the school. My picture was in the paper. I was finally *somebody.*

Dad returned home from Panama and saw me pitch the game that sent us to the playoffs. I remember looking at the guys who were picking on me, cocky with the confidence that success on the field brings, and thinking, *Remember me? Game on. No one else is gonna fight my battles now. You'd better watch out.*

The summer after my freshman year I played American Legion baseball. We had a pretty good team, but I felt I still had something to prove. My sister worked at the grocery store on the base as a bagger. After games or practices, I rode to the base with her, and she would drop me off at the gym. I was fourteen years old, and I started playing basketball against guys who played collegiate ball, guys who were twenty-five years old and ripped, guys who could dunk over me. I was a boy playing against men. *I will get good all by myself. I don't need those guys at school.* Guys at the base started looking for me, choosing me to be on their team, showing me stuff, helping me get better. I couldn't wait for my sophomore year.

When I wasn't playing basketball or baseball, I was busy digging myself into a hole with everyone else. Teachers didn't like my attitude. They prayed for me to be sick. I cheated on tests and couldn't stand to be under anyone's authority. My parents weren't sure what to do with me. The wall I had built around myself was ten miles high and five miles thick, and I was filling it with bitterness, anger, and rage. It got to the point at which I really didn't care what other people thought about me. I often got in trouble with some of my friends from the baseball team. We would go TP-ing (toilet papering) or egging or play pranks on the guys from the basketball team. My attitude and I were becoming significant issues wherever I went. At the time, I thought I knew everything. Looking back, I can see what an idiot I was.

My sophomore year began, and I was ready for basketball. I made the varsity team and played as a swinger. I practiced with the varsity and played every minute of the junior varsity games. After the JV game, I changed uniforms and sat the bench for the varsity games, playing a few minutes here and there. My perseverance had paid off.

Baseball season came in the spring, and we had a good team, going undefeated all the way to the playoffs. It was during baseball season that I finally started dating, but that didn't last too long. My first girlfriend called me one night and broke up with me. I was devastated. I felt lost and confused, bitter at the whole situation. *I'm a jock. I'm an athlete. This isn't the way it's supposed to happen.* Dad overheard the whole thing and approached me. We walked from home to church—a little over two miles—and he talked me through it. Our relationship had been damaged by his year away from home, but it was starting to heal—with a few significant collisions in the journey.

Like the times Dad kicked me out of the house.

I never drank alcohol when I was in high, and I never did drugs. Those weren't the things that tempted me. But I had a horrible, cocky, brash attitude, and sometimes it flared. By *flared* I mean I got completely out of control. When that happened, everything went red, and I just started punching things. I punched holes in doors and walls, broke things, and walked around in a sulking rage. Being a military man, Dad ran a strict house.

One winter evening I had disrespected him, breaking things in the house, and he kicked me out. There was snow on the ground, so I sat down and started putting on my shoes. Dad said, "What are you doing?"

I said, "You're kicking me out of the house. I'm putting my shoes on."

Dad replied, "I own those shoes. I paid for those shoes. Everything in here is mine. You're lucky I let you keep the clothes on your back. You're also lucky it's cold outside, or I'd make you walk down the street in your underwear."

I walked in the snow wearing a sweatshirt, sweatpants, and socks for a mile and a half to my friend's house. When I got there, I called the assistant basketball coach, who was also the school counselor, and told him that Dad had kicked me out of the house. The counselor drove thirty minutes to my friend's house to pick me up. He called Dad, but Dad didn't back down.

Eventually I learned my lesson, though it took Dad kicking me out of the house two or three more times. When I disrespected Dad, he kicked me out. There was always tough discipline, but underneath the discipline was a fierce love.

For two or three nights, I would end up staying at a friend's house—who happened to be Mom's best friend. I'm certain they called to check up on me, and when I was ready to humble myself and apologize, I was allowed to return home.

In retrospect, it probably wasn't the best way to deal with the situation. I certainly won't kick my sons out of my house. And if you were to ask Dad today, I doubt that he would say he felt he had done the right thing. I think he would probably confess to not handling everything perfectly. But it worked for us, and it got my attention enough to make me slow down and think.

For the record, Mom could hold her own as well. On one occasion I yelled at Mom, popping off at her, and she lifted me up and pinned me against the cabinets. She's only five-foot four, and she made it known without a shadow of doubt that she could handle me just fine. She also guaranteed that things would get worse for me when Dad got home.

The first two years of high school were rough years. But everything changed during my junior year.

FOUR

REDEEMED

"People don't like me because I'm mean and cocky and rebellious. Teachers don't like me because I smart off and don't care. I'm a punk, and I want to change. I want to live for God."

MY PARENTS sent me to a private Christian school instead of the public school in an attempt to protect me from some of the pressures of the popular teenage culture. But when it comes down to it, a Christian school for me wasn't much different from a public school—there were just chapel and Bible classes on top of everything else. In my small, competitive school of only six hundred kids, there were students who smoked and drank, and there were teen pregnancies.

When my junior year in high school started, I was ready. I wanted to continue to prove myself on the basketball court and on the baseball field. I wanted to let everyone know that I was someone to be reckoned with. Some people walk around with a chip on their shoulders; I walked around daring anyone to cross my path.

I went to church every Sunday while growing up. When I was in junior high, I committed and recommitted my life to Jesus at least five times, because we watched those Revelation movies about the end of the world—like *A Thief in the Night*—in Sunday School. Every time that movie or one like it was shown, I'd rush home and pray, because the "hell" was scared out of me.

I always knew about God while growing up. It wasn't as if I ever doubted His existence; it was just that I didn't really see how He affected my daily life, especially when it came to sports. Then, in the middle of my junior year, God caught me completely by surprise.

• • •

Two incidents took place near the beginning of the year that proved just how much I hadn't changed over the summer.

One day in class I was making fun of a girl who was one of Larisa's friends, and Larisa defended her. In the middle of class, Larisa stood up, pointed her finger at me, and said, "I'll never marry a guy like you." I was completely caught off guard. As coolly and nonchalantly as possible, I replied, "I don't care."

The second incident happened at the beginning of basketball season during the preseason tournament. I really respected my coach, Danny Beard. He pulled me aside before the season started and said, "Jeremy, you are our best scorer. But the rules apply to you just like everyone else. If you get two technical fouls, you're off the team."

I played dirty, and I played loud. I mouthed off at referees and yelled at players on the other team. I was cocky and I was good, and I wanted everyone to know it. We were at a preseason tournament, and I wasn't happy with the referees the whole game. I was standing at half court when the referee blew his whistle under the basket. He said, "Foul," and pointed right at me. I snapped immediately, yelling and trying to defend myself. *Technical foul number one.* The official season hadn't even started, and I already had one major strike against me. My coach took my side, even though he made me apologize to the referee. I was benched for the remainder of the tournament. I wasn't even allowed to suit up but watched the games from the stands with my parents.

I knew I had to change. I started talking with Coach Moore, the assistant basketball coach, and the school counselor, who knew me well. Coach Moore was familiar with my struggles and all the issues that I was dealing with. I wanted to change initially because I didn't want to watch any more games from the stands. I started reading Scripture, trying to find a way to improve myself—mainly so I could play sports. Coach Moore recommended some books on character and ways to deal with anger issues. Through all of this and for the first time, the Bible started to come to life for me.

Chapel is part and parcel of the private Christian school experience. One of my "enemies" from my freshman and sophomore year was Andy. This guy whom I despised was now without his friends who had all moved on to play basketball in some of the bigger high schools in hopes of being noticed and receiving basketball scholarships. In the absence of the other influences, Andy and I were becoming friends. Changes were also taking place in Andy's life, and he started getting involved in the chapel services, helping to lead worship.

Everyone was required to go to chapel. If you were cool, you sat in the back and did your best to ignore what was said and taking place on the stage. So there I was, sitting in the back, being cool, and Andy started singing "Whiter than Snow." As he was singing, I started crying uncontrollably. *What is happening to me? Everyone is looking at me.* I had no idea why the tears were flowing, but I couldn't stop them. God was using this song to rearrange the deep and hidden places in me. God was redeeming me, calling me, drawing me to Him. I had to get out of there.

I ran outside because I didn't want anyone else watching me blubber like an idiot. After Andy finished singing, he came outside to join me. "Dude, are you all right?" he asked.

I started confessing *everything.* I don't know why, and I couldn't have stopped it if I had tried. "People don't like me because I'm mean and cocky and rebellious. Teachers don't like me because I smart off and don't care. I'm a punk, and I want to change. I want to live for God. I don't even know what that means, but I'm ready to be different."

I held nothing back and opened my life to Andy, and as I was confessing to him, he started confessing back to me. Right then, for some reason, I looked up, and this beautiful white bird flew in and landed on the post near us and stared at us. The whole time we were talking, this bird was watching over us, and I realized that we were on holy ground. The very Spirit of God was moving in both our lives. Andy and I hugged, and for the first time I felt the powerful peace of God in my life. I truly believe that was the day God redeemed my life and began in me an intense lifelong journey of transformation.

And I began to change. Before the chapel incident, I wanted to change for *me*, so I could play sports. After that day I wanted to change for *God*, because I had tasted God's goodness, God's peace, and God's love. I wanted my life to truly mean something.

Even my coaches saw the changes that were taking place in me. I still played hard and aggressive basketball, but I wasn't mean. Right when everything seemed to be finally falling into place for me, the unthinkable happened—*technical foul number two.*

Whenever I play, I play with all my heart, with everything in me. That night the other team knew I was good, and they were doing whatever they could to keep me from scoring. Throughout the entire game one of the guys from their team was grabbing me, elbowing me, pushing me, and punching me. Finally he grabbed me around the neck, and I was sick of it. I drove my elbow into his head to get him off me and he crumpled to the floor. The referee, who didn't seem to be paying any attention to what the other guy was doing, saw what I had done, and he called the technical foul.

Out of fear, I looked at Coach Beard. Immediately I started to plead my case: "I didn't say anything, Coach.

He was punching me and had his arm around my neck." Coach Beard interrupted me and said, "Jeremy, I saw the whole thing. You don't have to worry about it—just relax. You're fine." He had seen the changes that were taking place in my life.

Baseball season came quickly, and we had an awesome year. We were undefeated heading into the playoffs and went all the way to the state championships. Everything in my life was going great.

One day I was looking at Larisa and said to her, "You look nice today." I had never seen her like that before. All of a sudden, she was beautiful. God was literally changing *everything*. She looked back at me and said, "You look nice too."

After baseball season finished, I approached Coach Orr again, who was also our class advisor. "Coach Orr, at one of our class meetings I want to apologize to the entire class for my behavior and attitude."

He took a long look at me and asked, "Are you sure you're ready to do that?"

"Yeah, I really need to say something."

Toward the end of the school year we held a class meeting to try to figure out how to do a fundraiser for our senior trip. I stood up before my entire class and said, "I'm sorry. I'm sorry for everything. I'm sorry for making fun of you. I'm sorry for disrespecting you. I'm sorry for being a jerk. I'm sorry that I teased some of you because you're not as athletic as I am, as if sports were everything. That's wrong, and I'm sorry. I want to change, and I just wanted you to know it and hear it from me."

Everyone sat in complete silence. Here I was, the school jock, confessing my bad behavior and stinking attitude and apologizing for all the wrong I had done. No one knew what to think or what to say. People actually wondered what was wrong with me.

I was finally headed in the right direction.

● ● ●

I knew at sixteen that God was stirring something in me—preparing me for some kind of journey. Yet I had no idea where it was going. As humans are questioning beings by nature, I started asking God some really big questions. *What did I do to deserve this? Why did you pick me? Why did you choose me? Where are you leading me?*

There's a word in the Scriptures that describes the process that God started in me: *metanoia*. It means "a change of mind," and it is the word that is often translated into English as *repent*. When Andy started singing in chapel that day, the Spirit broke through the walls I had built and the masks I had worn. God opened my eyes to see the sin in my life and created a hunger and thirst for Jesus Christ. I was made new. The old ways and patterns that once defined me did not define me anymore. I was changing because I had a new way of thinking; the mind of Christ was now in me.

He [Jesus] had equal status with God but didn't think so much of himself that he had to cling to the advantages of that status no matter what. Not at all. When the time came, he set aside the privileges of deity and took on the status of a slave, became *human*! Having become human, he stayed human. It was an incredibly humbling process. He didn't claim special privileges. Instead, he lived a selfless, obedient life and then died a selfless, obedient death—and the worst kind of death at that—a crucifixion (*Philippians 2:6-8,* TM).

Jesus had every right to claim a divine privilege and demand that others serve and follow Him. But instead of being a dictator, He led from a position of service and love. When He looked at people, He didn't see tax collectors, prostitutes, or sinners. He saw beautiful and broken children of God. He saw images of God that had been marred by sin and the struggles of life. He saw people God passionately loved, and Jesus' compassionate heart went out for them. Jesus served all people, allowing God's radical love to draw them to God.

God's Spirit completely caught me by surprise, opened my eyes, and helped me to see differently. The Holy Spirit began teaching me that people are valuable and beautiful because they are all created in God's image—a lesson that would later be reinforced when I made it to the major leagues. At the time, I couldn't begin to imagine or fathom the power of what had happened. And this was just the first step.

In order to follow Jesus, one must learn to give and learn to serve. But more important, in order to follow Jesus, one must learn to die to self. There's no place for the selfish in the kingdom of God.

For the first time in my life, I was passionately pursuing God for the sake of God himself rather than for the gifts He had given me. Then Larisa entered the picture.

FIVE

LARISA

WHEN A YOUNG COUPLE MAKES A VOW AND COMMITMENT TO ONE ANOTHER, THEY HAVE THE OPPORTUNITY TO LEARN HOW TO BUILD A DEEP AND MEANINGFUL LIFE TOGETHER.

MY HEART first skipped a beat in fifth grade. Her name was Rebecca. Every day after school I rode my bike as fast as I could to the crosswalk to catch a glimpse of her. When she rode by in her mom's car, I smiled and waved. I don't remember if she waved back or not.

I didn't have time for a girlfriend in junior high school. Everything in my world centered around sports: basketball, baseball, soccer, hunting. I wanted to be outside playing, exploring, running, throwing, and catching. A girlfriend took way too much time, and I had more important things on my mind.

The first girl I dated-—if that's what you want to call it—was during baseball season my sophomore year. She was the twin sister of my catcher and was also the first girl I kissed. When she called to break up with me, my heart was crushed. I must have been a bad kisser.

After God opened my spiritual eyes in chapel, and when Larisa and I were actually on speaking terms, we went on a date. It was nothing creative or fancy. We went to a park and simply talked. We started spending a lot of time together—until her friend stepped in. Larisa's best friend, the very one I had insulted earlier in the year, was still hurt. She didn't believe my apologies or see that I had started to change. She told Larisa not to date me anymore. Larisa was torn between me and her best friend. She finally sided with her friend and told me, "My best friend doesn't like you, and what she says means a lot to me. So we need to stop dating."

I was shocked, but at the same time I kind of understood. This was another consequence of my earlier behavior. I didn't get angry or try to defend myself, and I didn't criticize her friend. I sadly accepted the verdict. So Larisa and I went our separate ways.

The baseball season at school ended; we lost in regionals. I was now in the limbo season between basketball and school ball followed by summer American Legion ball. It was during this off-season time that I always focused on my studies at school.

Then Larisa called me at home. Dad answered and said, "Hey, that girl is calling."

"Jeremy, this is Larisa. I think it would be kind of cool to date you, to spend some time together and see what happens."

My parents had a long-established dating rule in my home. Basically, Mom and Dad interrogated anyone I had any interest in dating. It was almost like *Meet the Parents*—without the lie detector test. Larisa drove to my house and went on a long walk with my parents. I stayed at home. I was nervous and embarrassed for Larisa. When they returned from the walk, Mom and Dad said that everything was fine. Larisa thought the whole experience was really weird.

We spent the whole summer together before my senior year. Larisa came to all my baseball games, and we went out on dates afterward. I would drive her home and usually ended up getting home around midnight. I worked at Lefty's Bar and Grill at the airport to make a little spending money and to pay for my car insurance. I had to wake up at 4:30 A.M. to get there on time. But I loved spending time with Larisa and couldn't imagine a better way to spend the summer.

The first time I met Larisa's dad, Mark, I called him "Sir." I still call him "Sir" to this day. Mark owns a furniture company and is gifted in working with finances and numbers. It is the desire of his heart to support ministry efforts around the world. Mark taught me a lot about how to be a Christian and handle my finances. He stressed the importance of being grateful and faithful with the opportunities I have been given.

Paul writes that "the love of money is the root of all evil" (1 Timothy 6:10, KJV). Money in and of itself is a gift from God to be used responsibly, not hoarded selfishly. It takes money to build clean water wells, orphanages, and schools. It takes money to give the hungry something to eat and to clothe the naked. It takes money to provide all the services a victim of human trafficking needs for healing and hope for a future. God gives us money, and our calling and responsibility with money is to love our neighbor. But I'm getting ahead of myself.

One day when Larisa and I had been dating for about a month, I went over to her house, and Mark approached me. "Hey, man—I got something for you," he said. "It's over by the door." I looked, and right by the door was a brand-new set of golf clubs; Mark wanted me to be his golfing partner. He started taking me golfing, spending time with me. I wasn't very good at golf, but we enjoyed being together. Mark took Larisa and me to Mariners baseball games, and he would come with Larisa to watch my baseball games. We bonded pretty deeply.

My senior year was a time of discernment and decisions. I visited colleges and kept pursuing my dreams. Eventually I turned down a full-ride scholarship to Gonzaga for the opportunity to play professional baseball. Shortly after high school graduation, it was time to start making a living playing professional baseball.

Leaving was not easy. It was before the September 11, 2001, terrorist attacks, and Larisa went to see me off at the airport and was able to walk with me to the gate before I boarded the plane. She had bought me a new Bible and handed it to me at the gate. Giving me a hug and a kiss, she said, "Just don't forget about me." My eyes welled up with tears as she spoke. *This is it. My first time leaving.* After getting onto the plane, I kept my sunglasses on to look cool and hide the tears. Throughout the summer, I read and highlighted the Bible. Her dad also sent me a couple of books, encouraging me to have a positive mind-set, encouraging me to succeed.

That winter, after my first experience with professional baseball in the minor leagues, I came home to find a winter job. Mark hired me to work at one of his furniture stores, which was an hour's drive away. I worked hard, saved money, and continued seeing Larisa every chance I got. My dad had taken the initiative and moved me out of my room into the shop behind our house. He moved *everything*—my waterbed, my dresser—and said, "You're growing up now. It's time you take care of yourself. You're becoming a man, and you need your own place."

As Larisa and I became better friends, the voices started. At completely random times I would be bombarded with thoughts that I couldn't get out of my mind. *Dump her. Break up with her. Get rid of her. You don't need her. She's not the right one for you.* I had no idea where they were coming from, but they hounded me. These voices, these thoughts, were definitely not from God.

I remember sitting in the car with Larisa after a date when I finally decided to tell her what was happening. I told her I didn't understand what was going on and that I needed some space to figure everything out. We broke up, and she was devastated. It was two weeks before Christmas. I quit working for her dad and started lifting weights every day to get ready for baseball. I was working out to worship music, trying to find space to figure things out.

I continued hearing the voices, inundated with horrible thoughts. They started affecting my sleep, my attitude, even my appearance. Mom could tell that I was struggling, that I was hurting, even though I never said anything to her about what was happening in my head.

One cold morning I woke up at about 6:30, and there was a dark yet tangible image over me, choking me. I couldn't breathe and was struggling with this thing I can only describe as evil. I had no idea what was happening. Finally I struggled off the bed, jumped up, and ran outside in my sweats and t-shirt. Taking a deep breath, trying not to panic, I jumped into my car and called Mr. Orr, the counselor from high school, and told him that I had to talk to him. I met him at school and shared with him the thoughts that I had been having as well as the whole experience in the shop. Mr. Orr helped me begin to think through the whole situation, to gain perspective. But I was still terrified.

When I went back home, I did not want to go back to the shop, but I didn't feel that I could tell my parents the whole story. I told Dad that the shop was too cold and asked for permission to move back into the house. He was gracious and helped move me back in my old room.

Two days before Christmas Eve, I was driving home after working out at the gym, listening to worship music when I sensed God's whisper in my heart: *Keep on driving down the road.* I drove past my house and saw a road on the left. I turned onto it and pulled over to stop. Stepping out of the car, I started crying uncontrollably. There, in the middle of the snow, wearing shorts and a t-shirt, I fell to my knees. I called out to God and sensed the Holy Spirit saying to me, *Jeremy, you have placed Larisa on a pedestal. You have lifted her so high that you can no longer see me. I know you love her, and I want you to be with her, but I want it to be healthy. I want to be God of your relationship. I am God alone; I alone am worthy of your worship. No one else comes before me.*

After hearing from God in this profound way, I continued to worship God on my knees. The peace of His Spirit flooded over me. Opening my eyes, I saw that the snow around me had completely melted in a circle. I had experienced another holy encounter with Almighty God, this time in the middle of the snow.

I got back into the car and drove home. Mom greeted me and said, "You look good." I had a new countenance. God had once again drawn me into holiness and set me on the right path.

I immediately called Larisa to ask if we could meet to talk. She was still hurt and didn't know what to do. She finally agreed to go with me to Leavenworth, a little village a couple of hours away, where we could spend the day together.

I drove to her house, and her mom opened the door. She was not at all happy with me. In front of Larisa and tearing up, her mom grabbed me and said, "That is my little girl. Don't you dare hurt my little girl." Mark was there and just pretty much stayed out of it. Her mom was giving me the third degree to make certain that I knew my place.

Larisa and I drove to Leavenworth. We spent time ice skating and sharing hot chocolate. We had a good dinner and spent a lot of time talking. I told her *everything*. By God's grace, she understood. It was amazing. *She* was amazing. She came to my house to celebrate Christmas on Christmas Eve, and I went to her house for Christmas Day.

I was in love.

Shortly after Christmas, I reported to spring training. I was sent to play in Lansing, Michigan. Larisa came to visit me, to encourage me, and be near me. Unfortunately, I ended up having a horrible year in Lansing and got sent down to the Gulf Coast League. It was my first real experience with failure. After my discouraging year of baseball, I came home, and at the ripe age of nineteen, I bought an engagement ring.

Before I bought the ring, my agent sponsored me to go to the Pro-Athletes Outreach (PAO) conference. PAO equips professional athletes who desire to follow Jesus Christ to make a positive impact on the world in which we live. One night after the session concluded, I was lying in bed thinking about Larisa and clearly sensed God speaking to me again: *Marry Larisa.*

It took less than thirty seconds for me to get her on the phone. I told her, "Larisa, there's something I want you to know."

"What's that?"

"Well, I just wanted you to know that I love you."

"Oh, yeah, I know."

"No—listen to me. I want you to know that I truly, deeply love you."

"Oh," she said, catching her breath. "Wow."

I came home from the PAO conference, went straight to the jewelry store, and spent everything in my savings on a wedding ring. I have no idea how Dad knew what I did, but he knew. "Let me see it," he said when I walked in the door.

"See what?"

"I know you bought a ring—let me see it."

I showed him the ring, and he was impressed. Mom, on the other hand, wasn't excited at all. She thought we were too young to get married. Even though she and Dad married young, she wanted me to wait until I was older.

I wanted to ask Mark for permission to marry Larisa. I was really nervous as I went into his office. He looked at me and said, "Jeremy I don't know if you're going to

marry my daughter, but I wanted you to know that you have my blessing if you do." *How do dads know this stuff?*

• • •

It was her sister's sixteenth birthday. In retrospect, it probably wasn't the best timing, but I was only nineteen, and I didn't always consider the whole picture when I made decisions. Our old high school was having a basketball game against our biggest rival. A lot of people from our class were at the game, and I had worked with people at the school in planning the big engagement event.

At halftime we had staged a blindfolded free-throw contest. Larisa's name was pulled from the raffle to shoot the free throw. After she was blindfolded, a large banner was raised in front of the basketball goal. I sneaked out onto the court and got down on one knee. She shot the fake free throw, and people went crazy, cheering as though she had made a basket. She quickly took the blindfold off and couldn't believe what she saw, a huge banner that said, "Larisa, will you marry me?" It took her several seconds to figure out what was going on.

Then she looked at me and said, "Yes." The crowd cheered.

• • •

The year was 1999, and I was pitching for the Charleston (West Virginia) Alley Cats, the low-A affiliate of the Kansas City Royals. Larisa moved to Charleston to be near me, to come to my games, and to learn that there is nothing glamorous about minor league baseball. She got a job at Applebee's, and her dad rented her an apartment near our field. Mark has always taken good care of his baby girl. While I was living in an apartment without air-conditioning with four other guys, Larisa was living in an apartment with a window air-conditioning unit, cable television, and everything else she needed. My teammates and I would go hang out at her place every evening we weren't playing until she kicked us out before her bedtime. There was no cooler apartment in Charleston.

We went through premarital counseling with the chaplain from the Charleston team. Larisa got to know wives from the team and had a pretty good time getting acclimated to life in the minor league baseball world. I had a great year in Charleston, pitching really well. I even made the All-Star team.

After the season was over, in November, at the age of twenty, Larisa and I got married in a beautiful ceremony back home. We had a wonderful honeymoon in Tahiti. Our adventure as a couple was underway.

Getting married at a young age was a blessing in many ways. There are many people today who encourage waiting for marriage until you are established in your career and financially secure. Our self-focused culture advocates for young people to enjoy themselves, forego commitments while establishing and securing their futures. Our culture ridicules monogamous commitment. How unfortunate! When a young couple makes a vow and commitment to one another, they have the opportunity to learn how to build a deep and meaningful life together. I think that making a decision to commit to one another is related to finding meaning and purposeful lives.

Marriage is not easy. It is hard and requires sacrifice and commitment. The early years were a tremendous struggle for us. Together we learned to live off less than $1,000 dollars a month. Together we walked through these hard times. We survived the ups and downs of life. We did it together, and it shaped the kind of people and love mates we are today. Our faith and core values were established in the crucible of daily life together.

Today's Church needs to reach out to young couples and realize the potential for ministry to newlyweds. Those who have been married for fifteen years should mentor newlyweds, walking alongside them as they learn to build a faithful and healthy shared life. Too many young marriages end in divorce because no one teaches the couple how to endure the difficult times. Marriages built solely on sexual attraction and the emotions of late adolescence need to learn that love is a decision one makes every day. Husbands choose to love their wives by helping with the housework. A wife chooses to love her husband by cooking dinner. Both people learn to love each other by expressing gratitude and appreciation for everything the other person does. I'm not advocating gender-specific roles. What I'm saying is that love is a choice that manifests itself in the small things we do for each other on a daily basis.

Husbands, you are called to love your wife as Christ loved the Church. Out of the depths of His love, Jesus willingly gave His life for the Church. He didn't condemn or judge the Church—*He loved her.* Through His love, he freed the Church to be the hands and feet of God in the world. It is not the job of the husband to rule over his wife or to be a dictator. Christ's leadership took the form of a servant. Any husband who loves his wife like this will find that his wife will walk side by side with him through anything.

Because we were so poor during those early days, I made a promise to Larisa when we got married, "For our tenth anniversary, I will get you a better ring." Almost ten years later, shortly after I signed a multi-year contract with the San Francisco Giants, Larisa reminded me when she declared, "Yes! I'm getting the ring!" She had remembered my promise for ten years.

For our tenth anniversary, I wanted Larisa to know how much I appreciated all the sacrifices she made so I could play baseball. I wanted her to know that I loved her more now than I did when I called her from the PAO conference before we got engaged. I wanted her to know how grateful I was that God has placed her in my life.

To celebrate, both our families went to Maui. On our tenth anniversary we romantically renewed our vows. In a very simply service on the cliffs of Maui, I gave her a new ring. Grandparents took care of our son, and we celebrated a second honeymoon by spending four wonderful days together in paradise.

From the very beginning, God knew that it wasn't good for a man to be alone. God has so richly blessed me with Larisa to be my partner in life, to share in my successes and sorrows, and to help me continue to be the best me that I can be.

SIX

MOVING ON UP

I LOOKED UP TO SEE FUTURE
HALL OF FAMER JIM THOME
POINTING HIS BAT RIGHT AT ME.

Kansas City Royals Spring Training—Haines City, Florida, 2002

"Get Affeldt up."

It was close to the end of spring training, and we were playing the Cleveland Indians. Being the youngest on the team, I was a back-up, the grunt, there just in case they needed someone to pitch a few unimportant innings. The Royals management had already told me I was there to get some conditioning in and be with the veteran pitching staff in the bullpen, where they hoped I would pick up some good habits. It's hard to get psyched up for a spring training game, especially since I had little hopes of getting in a game, so I wasn't really paying attention when the phone rang.

"Get Affeldt up and ready—he's going in."

I started throwing to loosen up and warm up as quickly as I could. What seemed like a few seconds later, the pitching coach motioned me into the game. It was at that moment that I realized I was walking into a bases-loaded situation.

Come on, I thought. *These runners aren't my responsibility. If they score, it's not my fault. I just have to focus and give it my best.*

They handed me the ball, and I started rubbing it down. All of a sudden, the crowd went crazy. I looked up to see future Hall of Famer Jim Thome pointing his bat right at me. In 2001 he hit forty-nine home runs. My heart was pounding; I was scared to death.

Brent Mayne was the catcher and knew Thome's skills. I trusted Mayne and his calls from behind the plate. Mayne signaled for a first pitch fastball, and I blew it right by Thome for a strike. Then I threw a curveball, and he took it for strike two. Mayne called for a fastball inside, but I threw it a little too much inside for ball one. He called for a fastball away. *I'd rather throw another curveball*, I thought. But I trusted Mayne's experience. I threw the fastball right by Thome. I walked off the mound thinking, *I just struck out Jim Thome. That might be my only major league career strikeout, but it sure felt good.*

Tony Muser was the manager of the Kansas City Royals. He called me into his office and sat me down. "Kid, you made the team when you struck out Jim Thome."

My dream was coming true. I was actually headed to the major leagues. I called Dad, and he started to cry. I called Larisa, who had left spring training early to pack up stuff at home. She was preparing for me to be sent to Omaha for AAA. I told her that it was official: we were headed to Kansas City.

• • •

Senior Year in High School—Spring 1997

Scouts frequently came to my high school games during my junior year to watch one of my friends and fellow teammate play. While they were there watching him, they happened to notice my pitching ability. After a couple of games, a few scouts approached me and asked me to fill out some cards. I didn't have a clue as to who they were, but I did as they asked and never thought about it again.

On the first day of baseball practice my senior year, there were thirty scouts in attendance. I looked at my coach, and he nonchalantly said, "I didn't want to tell you. Just practice like normal." They stayed and watched the entire practice. Scouts were at every one of the games I pitched, and at some of those games there were more scouts than fans in attendance.

I started sending out videos to various colleges in hopes of playing collegiate ball and earning a scholarship. Washington State University contacted me and said I was overrated. Gonzaga showed interest throughout the season by attending almost every game I played.

I was interested in being an engineer if things in baseball didn't work out. I learned that LeTourneau University in Longview, Texas, had one of the best engineering programs. So Mom and I flew to Texas to visit LeTourneau and see if I could try out for the team.

I met the coach, told him that I was from Spokane, Washington, and very interested in playing baseball at LeTourneau. He invited me to work out and practice with the team that day. His son was the catcher for the team.

He asked me what pitches I threw. "Fastball, curveball, and a split-finger forkball."

"How hard do you throw?"

Scouts had been clocking me at ninety-one to ninety-two MPH consistently during games all spring.

"About ninety-one to ninety-two."

The catcher looked at me and laughed. "Yeah. Okay. Sure."

They put their All-American in to bat against me. I struck him out on three fastballs. They put in another player, and I struck him out too. I ended up striking out everyone I faced. They couldn't hit anything I was throwing that day. I played a little bit at first base and took batting practice as well. I even hit a couple of home runs.

After practice the coach invited me into his office. He said, "You are definitely welcome to play ball for us, but I won't be able to give you a sports scholarship. You've got good grades, so you can probably get an academic scholarship." Mom was definitely getting excited at this point, because this was my first real offer. And then he continued: "However, I want to be completely honest with you, Jeremy. I've written some books on baseball, and I've seen a lot of ball players in my time. I would love to have you play for us. I believe you could probably play for most NCAA Division 1 schools. In fact, if the word gets out, I realize that you may choose to play somewhere else.

But shooting straight with you, I don't think you have the ability or talent to play baseball professionally."

I stood up immediately, shook his hand, and responded, "Thanks. I'll get back to you."

Mom and I boarded the plane to head home. She was really excited, talking about filling out the paperwork and making plans to get everything arranged for me to move to Texas.

Finally, I looked at her and said, "Mom, I'm not going there— I'm not playing for LeTourneau." She looked at me, puzzled by my confident declaration. I continued: "Mom, I can't play baseball for a guy who can look me in the eye and say, 'I don't believe in you.' How can I play for a coach who has seen me only once and says that I can't achieve my dreams? I'm not playing for LeTourneau."

When I returned to school from Texas it was time for our baseball games to start. During my entire senior year I gave up just one earned run and allowed only five hits. I was actually frustrated because there was so little real competition. However, we ended up losing the game leading into the state championships because a mistake was made with the brackets. The team we had to play to qualify for the state championship was the other really good team in the state.

I had never pitched past the fifth inning in a high school game. By the fifth inning we were typically ahead by ten or more runs, and the mercy rule ended the game.

Now that we were facing the other top team in our state, the competition was intense. Neither team scored in the first seven innings of this state championship qualifying game.

One of our guys hit the ball hard, but their team made a great play and dashed our hopes. We went into extra innings to finish the game, and I pitched all the way to the ninth inning, when they finally scored five runs on me. I was exhausted by the time I was pulled and went home devastated after the loss.

After the game, a scout from the White Sox approached me and said, "Affeldt, you lost a lot of velocity during that game."

I defended myself and snapped back, "I haven't pitched past the fifth inning all year. I just threw one hundred sixty-five pitches." I got angry with him for what seemed to me to be a ridiculous and rude comment.

After the season ended, I was in Canada for our senior trip while the major league draft was taking place. If I were to be drafted, I knew it would happen within the first three rounds. I called home to see if any team had called, and my sister said, "The Royals just called; they drafted you in the third round."

"Who?" The only people I knew who played ball for the Royals were George Brett and Bo Jackson. I was drafted before my eighteenth birthday and signed with the Royals on June 18, less than two weeks after I turned eighteen. Gonzaga University had offered me a full-ride scholarship for four years to play for them. Much to Mom's dismay, I called them and turned down their offer.

I was headed to Fort Myers, Florida, to play rookie ball in the Gulf Coast League.

Gulf Coast League—1997-1998

The summer after I graduated from high school, I pitched in ten games and had a 2-0 record with a 4.50 earned run average (ERA). I returned to the Gulf Coast League the following year and continued to improve, going 4-3 with a 2.89 ERA. I earned my first promotion and was sent to play low-A ball in Lansing. It was in Lansing that I first experienced failure and discouragement, losing all three starts and carrying an ERA over 9.

Charleston, A Ball—1999

I continued to work, to learn, to grow, to persevere. During my third year in the minor leagues, I spent the entire season in Charleston, West Virginia, with the Charleston Alley Cats, surviving the heat and humidity by spending as much time as possible in Larisa's apartment. That summer I went 7-7 with a 3.83 ERA and was convinced that my career was headed in the right direction.

Wilmington, High-A Ball—2000

I set records while at Wilmington, North Carolina, but not the kind of records you want to be known for.

I set a record for giving up sixteen hits while pitching only five innings. The good news was that I gave up only three runs. It was part of the learning process. As long as I was throwing strikes, they were going to leave me in the game. The rest of the first half of the season didn't go much better.

One morning during the All-Star break, I was sitting and reading my Bible. I was complaining to myself. I wanted to quit. I was planning my exit from baseball when I noticed some notes stuck in my Bible that I had written at the PAO conference. The speaker had shared a story about a tandem bicycle. On a tandem bike there are two people who pedal and only one person who steers and brakes. The speaker related this image to the spiritual life. "Who is steering your bike?" he asked. "You should be working as hard as you can, not lazily waiting for something good to come your way. God is working with you and in you. The Holy Spirit alone should be steering, without any help from a back-seat driver."

As I read over the notes and remembered the story, I sensed God's whispered question: *Jeremy, where am I?*

I casually responded, *Well, of course, you are on the front.*

God questioned me again, *Am I?*

Then I started thinking about it. I wanted to be in control, and I wanted things to be going differently. I thought I knew what was best and was trying to do things on my own. I cried out to God, "Let me get out of the way and move to the back."

I became refocused and put quitting out of my mind. I worked as hard as I could the second half of the season, pitching really well and enjoying a solid second half, even though I threw seventeen wild pitches and led the entire Royals' organization and the Carolina League with sixteen losses to go with only five wins.

That off-season the Royals surprisingly protected me on their forty-man roster. The media had a field day with this, wondering why they would protect someone who lost sixteen games in high-A ball, but the Royals did not want to lose me to another team. I would be attending my first major league spring training the following year.

Wichita, AA Ball—2001

I ended up pitching only two innings in big league camp, and the Royals management assigned me to AA ball in Wichita, Kansas, for the year. Prior to arriving in Wichita, I started working with Mike Mason, and suddenly everything started clicking. My curveball became a pitch I could count on, and my location was vastly improving. The lesson of the tandem bicycle was still fresh in my mind as I continued reading my Bible regularly. I ended up making the AA All-Star team, the Texas League All-Star team, and the Post-Season All-Star team. I won ten games and carried a 3.90 ERA but still didn't get called up to play in the major leagues.

Beginning on September 1 and on through the end of the regular season, any player on the team's forty-man roster is eligible to play in an official regular season game. A lot of young players make their major league debut in September. There were others from my team who were getting called up to play. Not me. And I was very frustrated and angry.

I went home discouraged and defeated and had a small break before I had to report to the Arizona Fall League. I continued to pitch well in the fall league. The Royals kept me protected under their forty-man roster. Spring Training came quickly.

Spring Training—2002

I don't think anyone, including me, expected me to make the Royals' twenty-five-man roster heading into spring training. Spring Training was in Haines City, Florida, and I seemed to be hitting a really good rhythm with my pitching.

One day my general manager, Allard Baird, approached me and said, "Jeremy, I want you to give it all you've got to make this team." Shortly after he left, the AAA coach of the Omaha Royals came up to me and said, "When you're with me this year, I need you to work as hard as you can so you can get to the big leagues as quickly as possible." He started telling me all of his expectations, and I was confused. "You said 'when I'm with you this year,' but the Royals General Manager just told me to try to make the major league roster. Which one is it?"

I headed back to my locker to try to think things through. In the quiet God whispered, *They have only a pencil; I have the pen. Do not worry about things beyond your control. I am in control, and what I want to happen will happen.*

Our spring training games started. One day I was warming up in the bullpen to pitch against the Pittsburgh Pirates. The manager had called down to the bullpen, and the other pitchers in the bullpen started teasing me. "Have you ever pitched in a big league game before?" I told them that I pitched a couple of innings last year, which only encouraged their laughter. I got called into the game, and all of a sudden I started throwing as I had never thrown before. My fastball was 94-95 MPH. In the two innings I pitched, I struck out five of the six guys I faced. Heads were turned.

Joe Posnanski, a sports writer for the *Kansas City Star*, was at the game and wrote a huge story about me, noting that he had been experiencing a boring spring training game when this mediocre prospect from nowhere came in and started pitching. *And then he really started pitching.* You could tell by the way the ball popped in the catcher's mitt that he was throwing the ball hard. A scout sitting near Posnanski said, "The kid ain't Koufax. But for two innings, Koufax couldn't have been any better." Joe turned to Allard Baird and asked him point blank, "How are you going to keep this kid off the team?"

Allard looked at Joe and with a sly smile replied, "Who said he's off the team?"

In fourteen spring training innings, I had fourteen strikeouts and a 0.64 ERA.

I struck out Jim Thome in the last spring training game, and Muser confirmed what Posnanski had written: I deserved a place on the team.

Traveling on the team plane was an experience in and of itself. I had an entire row to myself. And there was steak to eat. I actually had to go buy a suit to travel. When the plane landed in Kansas City, I went straight to the clubhouse. *This is the coolest thing ever.* Two lockers down, Mike Sweeney was watching me and laughing at me. Sweeney told me, "You'll get used to it, kid."

In order to reach the places we desire, the Holy Spirit often leads us through deserts and valleys and seasons where we must learn to trust only in God. My journey was unfolding into a new adventure.

SEVEN

The Royals knew that I was not only
effective as a starter but also did well
coming out of the bullpen.
They approached me and asked me
if I would be the closer.

Kansas City Royals, Rookie Season—2002

After dramatically striking out Jim Thome in spring training, I made the team as a reliever. I made my major league debut on April 6 against the Chicago White Sox. Pitching two innings, I gave up three hits, a run, and recorded my first strikeout in a 14-0 loss.

A couple of weeks later, against the Detroit Tigers, the game was tied at two in the sixth inning. Chris George had pitched well but was tiring quickly. With one out and the lead run on second, manager Tony Muser motioned for me to come into the game. I pitched the remainder of the game, striking out five and walking one. I retired eleven of the twelve guys I faced and recorded my first professional win.

Mike Sweeney was the captain and hero of the Kansas City Royals. He modeled leadership through a humble and encouraging attitude, caring for all the guys on the team. Sweeney played his heart out every night. From day one, he took me under his wing and showed me the ropes. I watched how he encouraged everyone he came into contact with. I observed how he led in the clubhouse, on the field, and off the field. Everyone loved Mike Sweeney. I even saw him hugging umpires. One of the best things that happened to me while playing for the Royals was developing a friendship with him. In so many ways he mentored me on how to play in the major leagues and avoid the temptations that could ruin me. Many players have thrown their careers away because they made bad choices. There are many people who hang around hoping to befriend professional athletes, stroking their egos and presenting activities that can ruin a player's reputation and get him into trouble. Sweeney and I watched each other's backs. One season we even roomed in adjoining rooms and kept the door between open. We held each other accountable to live our daily lives with integrity. To this day, I have a genuine love for that Mike Sweeney and his family.

My time as a reliever didn't last very long. Less than two months into my first major league season, the Royals decided to develop me into a starting pitcher. I was put on a pitch count to develop stamina and got my first start against the Baltimore Orioles. I pitched four innings, gave up a run, and earned a no-decision in a 4-3 loss. I didn't adjust very quickly to starting. Over the next two months I started seven games, officially losing four of them and racking up an ERA over 5.

In June the St. Louis Cardinals came to Kansas City for an interleague series. In one of the games I was pitching, we were down a run going into the fourth inning when everything changed. Over the previous few weeks, before the Cardinals came to town, a blister had developed on the middle finger of my pitching hand. The middle finger is your control finger and absolutely necessary for being effective as a pitcher. Sometime in the fourth inning, the blister popped. I wiped my finger off on my uniform. My once-white uniform now had blood stains all over it. Every pitch I threw hurt worse than the one before. I couldn't finish my pitches and started walking hitters, leaving pitches up, which is always dangerous. I was taken out of the game.

I was diagnosed with "pincer nails." Instead of growing straight out, my fingernails were growing down into my skin. The pressure and friction from pitching were tearing my finger apart. As I squeezed the ball, the nail pushed on the skin, digging into my nail bed, tearing the skin and filling with blood. When the blisters popped, raw skin and nerves were exposed. The pain was excruciating.

The team doctors discovered not just one blister but three stacked on top of each other. Because of the location of the blisters, I couldn't pitch and was placed on the disabled list. The Royals knew that if I continued to pitch with the blisters I could end up hurting my arm. I ended up missing forty-eight games of my rookie season.

The blisters were cut out, and we let the finger heal. I made three rehab starts for Wichita and returned to the Royals the first week of August, pitching a perfect inning against the Twins. But it wasn't too long before the blisters resurfaced. The Royals sent me to the disabled list for a second time. They wanted me to make sure that the blisters were completely taken care of before I returned. When I finally came back, I was put in the bullpen and used as a set-up man. The Royals lessened my pitch count and closely monitored my throws.

Halfway through the season, Tony Pena replaced Tony Muser as the manager. In the off-season, Pena sent me to the Dominican Republic to play winter ball. While I was there the blisters returned. Pena told me to soak my hand in garlic juice to toughen up the skin. A callous formed on my finger. But the callous quickly hardened and tore, and more blisters remained underneath. Even though I had great numbers in the Dominican Republic, I was in incredible pain. Finally I took a picture of my finger with my cell phone and sent it to the trainer in Kansas City. He showed the picture to Pena, who said, "Enough." They ended my winter season.

Kansas City Royals—2003

Going into spring training for my second year with the Royals, I felt really good and was throwing the ball very well. I had a great spring and ended up battling Runelvys Hernandez for the first spot in the starting rotation. Tony Pena was still the manager and couldn't decide who should start opening day. In the end, he flipped a coin, and I lost. Runelvyz got the start against the Chicago White Sox and ended up throwing a shut-out, 3-0.

And then the blister returned, after only four games, and I was placed back on the disabled list. To say I was discouraged and frustrated would be a huge understatement. My career was being hijacked by a stupid blister. A couple of weeks passed, and everything appeared good. I returned to the Royals at the beginning of May as a starter and put together a string of solid outings.

On July 23 against the Minnesota Twins, I got my final start of the year. I pitched five complete innings, good enough for the win, and had another quality start, giving up three hits while striking out five; but the blisters were coming back. Once again, I was shuffled to the bullpen, a move I was told was only temporary. While in the bullpen, against the Tampa Bay Devil Rays, I earned my first save.

I was on an emotional roller coaster. The whole ordeal was a humbling, irritating, and frustrating experience. I was being given the chance to live out my dreams, and I couldn't pitch because of a blister on my finger. Larisa encouraged me and supported me to the best of her abilities. I knew that she was frustrated and questioning as well, but she faithfully walked with me through everything. I prayed almost nonstop but heard very little in response.

In order to pitch, I had to put fake skin on my finger and reapply it regularly. On one occasion, we actually had to buy skin cells to make the skin on my finger grow back. It was a demoralizing cycle that tested my will to continue playing the game. The media began labeling me "injury-prone," which didn't help my image in the eyes of the community.

On August 21 the Royals announced that I would be spending the rest of the season in the bullpen. I finished the year with a 7-6 record—four saves, one hundred twenty-six innings pitched, and a 3.93 ERA. As a team, we had our only winning season for the first decade of the new millennium.

Kansas City Royals—2004

During the off-season I was determined to take care of the nail problem once and for all. I went to see a specialist in Illinois. He looked at my fingers, diagnosed the pincer nails, and said he knew of a doctor in Kansas City who specialized in fingers. *The solution was in KC the entire time.*

I set up an appointment with the doctor. He did have a solution, but it came with significant risk.

"We need to remove one-fourth of your fingernail. We'll pour acid onto the nail bed, and it will never grow out again. This will completely eliminate the nail growing downward. The risk is that you could lose feeling in that finger."

I knew that if I lost the feeling in that finger I would never be able to pitch effectively again. However, I didn't hesitate at all and told the doctor that I was ready to take the risk and have the surgery.

At the beginning of spring training there was some tenderness with my finger. It took a few outings to toughen up the skin, but soon everything started falling into place. I was starting again and pitching deep into games. I was learning how to pitch effectively at the major league level, keeping our team in the game.

And then our closer went down. Mike MacDougal, who could throw the ball one hundred-plus miles per hour and had a breakout year in 2003, was struggling with flu-like symptoms all spring. He lost weight and velocity and was sent to the minor leagues to recover.

The Royals knew that I not only was effective as a starter but also did well coming out of the bullpen. They approached me and asked me if I would be the closer. I was torn. I wanted to start and felt that I was doing a good-quality job as a starter. But I also wanted to be a team player.

Once again I moved back to the bullpen.

It didn't take long for me to hit my stride in the bullpen. I didn't have to pace myself for an entire game and could go full bore for an inning or two. I was throwing the ball up to ninety-nine MPH, something that's not common for left-handed relievers.

One day I was playing catch in the outfield, throwing the ball the way I had been throwing it for the past twenty years of my life, when all of a sudden there was a tremendous amount of pain down my right side. I had no idea what it was and was determined not to let it affect me. The Royals didn't put me on the disabled list but rested me for a week.

The week passed. Interleague play had started, and we were playing St. Louis again. I went in to close a game and was pitching to Reggie Sanders. As I was throwing a fastball, it felt as if someone had shot me in the side. The ball almost hit Reggie in the head. He glared at me, and I felt horrible. On the next pitch, I grimaced and doubled over on the mound from the pain. Sanders singled up the left side. I was choking back tears.

The Royals sent me to get an MRI. The official diagnosis was a three-centimeter tear in my right oblique. I was placed back on the disabled list and effectively shut down for six more weeks.

Frustration reigned in my soul. I cried out to God on a regular basis, determined that in my persistence and perseverance He would respond. *God, what is going on? Now I'm hurt again, this time with something completely different. I was just starting to find my stride, but every time I begin to achieve success, I end up back on the disabled list. What do you want me to do?*

Eventually, the oblique healed, and I finished the season as the closer, earning thirteen saves. The off-season came, and with it came my first lesson in salary arbitration.

Arbitration is a miserable experience.

The lawyer representing the team basically tries to portray how untalented and worthless you are, defending the salary that the team would like to pay you. When I went to arbitration the Royals labeled me a "lefty specialist," not as a starter or a closer but as a pitcher who comes in only to face left-handed hitters. This hadn't been my role on the team, and it immediately diminished my value in the eyes of the judge. Their lawyer actually stated, "The reason more fans don't come to games in Kansas City to watch the Royals play is that they can't stand to watch you pitch." The attorney attempted to obliterate my abilities in every way possible. He didn't even know the number of my jersey but looked at the black-and-white statistics and interpreted them in way that fit his agenda: "Mr. Affeldt just isn't a very good pitcher!"

What was really ridiculous about the process was the reality that we were only $50,000 apart in negotiations. One of my agents looked at him and said in my defense, "If he's so bad, why are you giving him this much money in the first place?"

The team's lawyer misrepresented the facts throughout the entire proceeding. The union could have lied in my defense, but I told them ahead of time, "If you lie, if you dare fabricate my statistics, I will get up and walk out. I will take a loss. Do not lie."

Allard Baird, the general manager, wasn't present at my hearing. I think he knew they were going to lie.

They were saying stuff that wasn't even close to the truth, determined to win this case at all cost. I was shocked at their tactics and behavior. In the end, the Royals won the arbitration case.

After the process was over, representatives of the Royals came to me and said, "Jeremy, it's nothing personal; this is just how the baseball business works. We had to win this case." It felt as if I had been stabbed in the back.

During my entire career with the Royals I did everything I was asked to do. I still believe the main reason they sent me to the bullpen was that they didn't want me to continue as a starter. The Royals didn't want to recognize me as a starter in the arbitration procedure.

Frustrated and angry, I turned the negativity into determination. I spent the off-season working out and preparing for the next season. I had something to prove.

EIGHT

A ROYAL PAIN: PART 2

ONCE AGAIN, MY GOOD FRIEND MIKE SWEENEY
HAD MY BACK. I BELIEVE HE PRETTY-MUCH
SAVED MY CAREER.

Kansas City Royals—2005

While I was working out in the off-season, I felt a pop high up in my leg. For a couple of days I could barely walk. I love hunting in the off-season, but I was in too much pain. I couldn't lift weights. I visited with the trainer in Kansas City and told him that my leg was killing me. He diagnosed it as a strain and told me to keep a close watch on it.

One of the first things the Royals told me when I arrived for spring training was that they wanted me to start again. *Really? I can't believe this*. The business side of baseball has a way of stealing a player's joy and love for the game. My leg was still tender, and because of the injury the Royals decided to keep me as a closer instead of waiting for my leg to heal.

Early in spring training I was called in to close a game. While I was following through with my delivery, I pulled my groin muscle. *Great. Another injury. You've got to be kidding*. I spent the majority of the spring in rehabilitation mode. Thankfully, the healing processes worked quickly, and I was able to pitch by the start of the season. The muscle was a little sore, but I could live with it.

I was given my first save opportunity against the Detroit Tigers. My fastball was only eighty-eight MPH. The coaches came out to visit with me on the mound. "What's going on? What's wrong?"

"Nothing," I replied, "My groin hurts a little, but it's nothing."

I was placed on the disabled list for another six weeks. I developed a terrible attitude, and I was an emotional wreck. I'm very competitive, and I want to be in the game. I want to do my part. I want to make a difference for the team. There's no way I can do that on the DL.

After six weeks and a couple of rehabilitation stints in Omaha, I returned to the Royals on June 4. I had lost my position as the closer, because Mike MacDougal was closing well in my absence. He was a good friend, and I was happy for his success. However, I was eager to pitch well and prove myself—to find my place and role on the team. But things didn't go as I had planned.

While in Arizona for an interleague series playing the Diamondbacks, I was brought in to pitch against Troy Glaus. I was feeling really good, throwing the ball hard and accurately, getting guys out. As I pitched to Glaus, my leg popped. I was so frustrated that I didn't tell anyone.

One of the other pitchers on the team noticed that something was different and asked me about it. I didn't admit anything. He took me to look at the video of me pitching. He pointed out that I was using only my upper body to throw. He confronted me: "You might be throwing hard, but you're not throwing right. You're slinging the ball. You're losing all the power in your legs. You're going to ruin your arm and your career."

I was still determined to keep it to myself. Even after he confronted me, I didn't say anything. Thankfully, he went to management on my behalf.

Management called me in and asked me what was wrong. I told them that I felt a pop high in my leg when pitching to Glaus and that it still hurt. At first they didn't believe me but sent me anyway to get another MRI. The MRI report that came back shocked everyone. "He has completely torn one of his groin tendons. There are supposed to be three, and we can find only two. At the top of your leg there's a complete tear, and the tendon has rolled somewhere down your leg. We can't find it anywhere on the MRI."

Then the doctor said, "His body basically performed its own surgery. We would have done it to relieve the pain, but now that it's torn, he'll be fine in a week; there's no need to put him on the disabled list."

They put me on the list anyway.

Fifteen more days of waiting, even though five days after meeting with the doctor I felt fine.

I finally returned to the Royals on July 7. The rest of the season was a roller coaster. Through the end of July, my ERA was only 2.18. But a monster in August was about to pounce on me.

We were playing the New York Yankees at historic Yankee Stadium. We had a comfortable lead going into the ninth inning, and I was brought in to finish the game.

We were ahead 7-3 and only three outs away from victory; a good and needed road win.

With a runner on first and one out, Jorge Posada grounded a ball right back to me—perfect for a game-ending double play. I spun to throw the ball to second, stepped on the rosin bag, and threw the ball into center field. The Yankees rallied and ended up winning 8-7. I started to apologize to Royals Manager Buddy Bell and explain about the rosin bag. He said he didn't want to hear any excuses and exploded at me; I accepted full responsibility for the loss in my talks with the media.

The very next day Zack Greinke was pitching, and the Yankees were hitting him hard. Losing 5-1 in the fifth inning, Buddy called me into the game. Frustrations from the previous day carried over. I figured that Buddy was trying to teach me a lesson. I was on the mound, but I was not really pitching, just throwing the ball as hard as I could. A couple of runs scored, but they were credited to Greinke. I came back out for the sixth inning and gave up three runs of my own.

After finishing the sixth inning, I headed into the dugout, looked at my pitching coach, and said, "If you're just going to use me as a mop-up guy, if I'm not a set-up or a closer, then you should leave me in the game."

I got ready to sit down when Buddy motioned to me and said that I was done for the day. I started walking up the tunnel to the clubhouse when out of nowhere Buddy came aggressively running up, got in my face, and started yelling at me. "Affeldt, do you have a problem with me?"

"Yeah, I've got a problem with you!"

And there in the tunnel, in the presence of the New York media, an enormous fight began. My friend and teammate Matt Stairs heard us yelling at each other and came flying up the tunnel, positioning himself between me and Buddy. Stairs grabbed me and told Buddy to get back to the dugout and manage the game. Stairs then pushed me up the tunnel toward the clubhouse. Buddy followed us into the clubhouse and kept yelling.

"What I ought to do right now is punch you," he said. "But you're not man enough to be punched."

I absolutely lost it. At that point I didn't care about baseball. I didn't care about the Royals or pitching. I didn't care about anything. The frustrations and anger of the past four seasons exploded out of me. I completely lost control and said, "Well, then, I'll make myself man enough," and took a swing at my manager. Stairs blocked the punch, grabbed me, and yelled at Buddy to get back to the team.

On his way out, Buddy continued to mouth off about my attitude. The closest thing to me was a chair. I picked it up and fired it at him. The chair bounced off a pole right next to Buddy's head, just missing him. He left.

Stairs pinned me and got me to sit down, telling me not to come back to the bench. Glancing around, I saw my general manager, Allard Baird, three feet to my left. He had witnessed the whole thing. I started yelling at him, too. "This is all your fault!"

In the clubhouse that day were Zack Greinke, my general manager, our traveling secretary, and three generations of New York Yankees clubhouse attendants. Greinke said he was scared to death of me. The clubbies said they had never witnessed anything like that, ever.

We lost the game. I got onto the plane, seething with anger and hurt. I didn't say anything to anyone. I didn't look at anyone. I texted Larisa and said, "I'm pretty sure I'm getting released. And I know I deserve it."

Once again, my good friend Mike Sweeney had my back. I believe he pretty-much saved my career. He approached Buddy and Allard and set the record straight.

After I had left the game and had started walking up the tunnel, Buddy looked at my pitching coach and asked what I said to him. The pitching coach looked at Buddy and *lied to his face*. The pitching coach replied, "Jeremy said that you don't know what you're doing, that you're a terrible coach." Sweeney looked at the pitching coach, and his mouth dropped. He couldn't believe what he was hearing. Of course Buddy wanted to challenge me. Of course Buddy wanted to confront me. *But I had never said those words.*

Sweeney confronted the pitching coach, who just walked away, seemingly oblivious to everything that was going on. When he boarded the plane, Sweeney took Buddy and Allard aside and told them the truth about what had happened.

The very next day we were back in Kansas City, and I went in to meet with Buddy at the stadium. "Who do you think you are to talk to me like this?" Buddy was still fuming and understandably so.

"Buddy, with God as my witness, I didn't say those things."

Buddy replied, "You leave God out of this."

"Buddy, I can't leave God out of this. God's everywhere. I'm supposed to be acting like a follower of Jesus Christ, and I've been doing a terrible job. I represent Him wherever I go, even when I screw things up. I'm apologizing to you, and I'm apologizing to God; I was wrong. But Buddy, I can't leave God out of this."

Immediately everything calmed down. Like two grown men are supposed to do, Buddy and I were able to talk through everything. It was a healing experience.

Finally, Buddy asked me, "Jeremy, what do you need?"

I said, "I need someone who will work with me. The pitching coach we have is not helping me. I don't think he likes me, and he's been messing up my mechanics. I'm getting worse, and I'm completely lost on the mound."

"Who do you want?"

I said, "I need Mike Mason."

The very next day Mike Mason was in Kansas City. Buddy was the only guy who knew about it. Every morning I worked with Mason at Mac 'n Seitz, a local baseball training facility. After working with Mason, I would go to the stadium and work some more at the field. Buddy knew I was working hard, so he tried to get me into games as much as possible. For the rest of the season Buddy became a father figure to me. He helped to salvage what had been an awful second half of the season.

In the final two weeks of the season, everything started to come around. Mason helped me develop a change-up, and I started dominating hitters again. I pitched twelve innings over the final two weeks and didn't give up a single run.

At one point during that August, when things were so bad I wanted to quit, I remember sitting on the counter at our apartment, crying and telling Larisa, "I don't want to do this anymore. They're changing my role so much, I'm getting hurt all the time, and we just keep losing. It's no fun. I want to be done. I really want to quit."

But Larisa wouldn't let me quit. She reminded me of what I had said when speaking to so many young people about chasing dreams and persevering through trials. She reminded me of what it meant to be an example in the public eye who walked faithfully through challenging difficulties. She helped me to refocus and remember why I played ball.

Thankfully, the final two weeks helped keep the entire season from being a disaster, although it wasn't really reflected in the statistics. My numbers for the season were bad. I pitched only forty-nine innings with no wins, no saves, a dozen holds, and a 5.25 ERA.

It was time to go to arbitration again. This time I didn't even put up a fight.

Kansas City Royals, first half of the season—2006

I returned to the starting rotation at the beginning of 2006, being named the third starter by the end of spring training. In nine starts, however, I won only two games and racked up a 7.80 ERA. My final major league start came against the New York Yankees. I surrendered ten runs on eleven hits in a 15-4 loss.

Back to the bullpen.

I like to read. On most game days I'll sip a coffee in the morning and read for an hour or two. Toward the beginning of the 2006 season a friend gave me the book *Pain, Perplexity, and Promotion: A Prophetic Interpretation of the Book of Job,* written by Bob Sorge and published by Oasis House.

I'm thinking, *I don't need to read about Job; I know his life was worse than mine.* Still, I told my friend that I would read it, and I kept my word.

My first four years in major league baseball were a struggle. I regularly visited the disabled list and had lost favor with fans and the organization. In four years we had only one mildly successful season as a team. In the introduction to the Book of Job, the accuser approached God and said, "Job worships you only because he's got everything he could possibly want. How does he react when the bad things come?"

Alan Redpath, a British evangelist, pastor, and author, once said, "When God wants to do an impossible task, he takes an impossible man and crushes him."

Through the pain and the struggles, God was preparing my heart, breaking me of my selfishness and arrogance. God was drawing me close, creating in me a greater passion to live out my faith in such a way that the love and servant leadership of Jesus would be transparent in everything I did. For years I wanted to be someone who helped young people navigate the challenges placed before them in our culture. I wanted to be identified as someone who helped people deeply and not just as a baseball player. God was birthing big dreams in me.

God was teaching me to seek the ways of Jesus Christ, and His inexplicable peace began to permeate my life once again. Through the struggles I had endured, the Holy Spirit was protecting me, even as I wrestled and wondered where God was and what He was doing.

I had such a small perspective. I was too fixated on the things right in front of me. I was so blinded by tears of pain that I didn't see God's smile. My faith was so small that I struggled to trust that He was still working in my life. David wrote the most beautiful, heart-wrenching psalms while walking hand-in-hand with pain and struggle. God was leading me through the valley of death so that I would know the fullness and beauty of what it meant to really live life with Him.

Following Jesus begins when we take up our cross. The cross is the epitome of pain, brokenness, humiliation, and despair. The way of the cross is not a carefree way, but it is the only way that leads to real life. God was walking with me as I learned to carry my cross. I just didn't understand it at the time.

I pitched well in the bullpen, even though I was being used in an irregular way. On May 31 Allard Baird was fired as the general manager and replaced by Dayton Moore. We had a new pitching coach, Bob McClure, who told me that other teams were looking at me. He let me know they were pitching other people in my role to figure out who could do what for the Royals in case I was traded.

Late in July, as the trade deadline was approaching, we were playing the Texas Rangers. I was brought in with the bases loaded in a tight game and got the needed out. As we got onto the plane to head back to Kansas City, I remember praying, *God, please give me a fresh start. Give me a second chance.*

July 31 came, the day of the trade deadline. Buddy told Dayton that I had the stuff to do well in the majors but that I needed to get out of Kansas City to make it happen. Five minutes before the deadline ended, Matt Stairs was traded to the Rangers. And thirty seconds after that, Dayton Moore called me and informed me that I was being traded to Colorado.

Larisa packed my bags and met me at the airport. I drove to the stadium to get my things and say good-bye. Dayton Moore walked me out and said, "This is good for you." He wrote a nice letter on my behalf and sent it to Colorado.

My prayers were answered.

NINE

SEVERAL SPORTSWRITERS LATER COMMENTED
THAT BARRETT HAD SUCCESSFULLY BLOCKED
THE PLATE, BUT BOTH THE PADRES MANAGER
AND THE FIRST-BASE UMPIRE AGREED WITH
THE SAFE CALL. WE WERE OFFICIALLY
HEADED TO THE POST SEASON.

Colorado Rockies, second half of the season—2006

The plane landed in Denver, and I went straight to the stadium, found the clubhouse, and got dressed. I walked out to the bullpen just as our starter was running to the mound to begin the game. *Purple pinstripes. Surrounded by mountains. This is surreal.*

Two days after the trade deadline I got my first game action as a member of the Colorado Rockies. They brought me in to pitch the ninth inning in a game against the Milwaukee Brewers; we were leading 8-1. I was pitching to Prince Fielder with two strikes, I threw a curve ball, and he hit a one-handed pop-up. It kept going and going and eventually left the park. *My very first opportunity in my new beginning—and I gave up a home run?* Fans started yelling at me, "Welcome to Coors Field!" The ball really does carry well when you're a mile above sea level. The remainder of the 2006 season with the Rockies didn't get much better.

Statistically speaking, it was my worst season. I finished with eight wins, eight losses, one save, and a 6.2 ERA. Pitchers with 6.2 ERAs usually get released and find themselves looking for a job the next season. My agent called and said that Colorado had offered me a raise for the next year. *I couldn't believe what I was hearing.* I took the offer without hesitation.

Colorado Rockies—2007

Going into spring training, I had been introduced to the world of sports psychology by my agent, who gave me the book *Golf's Sacred Journey: Seven Days at the Links of Utopia*, by David L. Cook and published by Zondervan. In the book, a mentor and coach named Johnny teaches a golf professional powerful lessons about unleashing his true potential as a player and as a human being. Using many settings on and off the course at Utopia, he shares the secrets of a lifetime about significance and leaving a legacy. The book teaches valuable lessons about the mental aspect of any game, and I started taking notes to apply to my pitching.

In Romans 12:2 and Ephesians 4:22-24 the Scriptures talk about a renewing of the mind—that the attitude of our minds is to be made new, and that was what was happening to me at the deepest level of my mind, heart, and soul. I knew about loving God with my heart, but I was learning to love God with my mind (see Matthew 22:37). My thought processes were changing. I was learning to see the good that surrounded me, appreciating the *beautiful* and *noble*, the *worthy* and the *admirable*. My prayers changed from self-centered to confessing and declaring the goodness and greatness of God. Through the Scriptures, life circumstances, and the book from my agent, God was growing me into a passionate follower of Jesus Christ—and a leader.

Leadership does not mean simply reflecting one's surroundings. Leaders help create a healthy, positive environment wherever they are. The heart of a leader is created through trials and sufferings. Perseverance and a focused determination toward significant ends create meaning in the mundane, daily grind. Leaders know that it is impossible to be successful in a negative environment.

When I played for Kansas City, it was often a struggle to come to the ballpark. A tangible negative atmosphere permeated everything. When guys were called up from the minor leagues to play for the Royals, I would overhear them saying that they had more fun in AA or AAA than in the big league with Kansas City. They actually preferred playing in the minor leagues over playing in the major leagues! The fact that Mike Sweeney consistently worked and encouraged a positive mind-set in the middle of so much losing is a testimony to his character and integrity.

Leaders also surround themselves with friends who are encouraging and supportive, who deeply believe in one another. A leader doesn't cast a selfish vision for followers but instead partners with friends who share dreams and goals to achieve together. Everyone involved grows; each one helps you, and you help each of them be the person God created him or her to be.

When I joined Colorado, I became part of a team where the majority of players and the management actually believed in one another and worked and played for one another. We wanted to be our best for each other. I came to the clubhouse enjoying my teammates, enjoying the game. When we traveled on road trips, we did things together. The most fragmented thing that might happen is that one group might go out for sushi. We were a band of brothers who believed in each other. Winning seemed to flow naturally out of the environment we worked hard to create.

I found a good rhythm that season with the Rockies. I was being used primarily as a lefty-specialist. I carried an ERA close to 2 through my first fifty games and didn't give up a home run until August. For the first time in my career I had the chance to make the playoffs, but I had no idea that we would do it in such historic fashion.

"The Streak"—winning twenty-one out of twenty-two games

We had an unbelievable lineup. As we entered September, everyone was playing really well. My teammates were getting on base, stealing bases, and hitting homers. Our pitching was flat-out unhittable and intimidating. But going into September, we were also seven games behind division-leading Arizona and in a wild-card fight with San Diego and Los Angeles as well.

"The Streak," as it is now known, started on September 16 against the Florida Marlins. In that game Todd Helton hit the three hundredth home run of his career, and we had an 11-0 lead after five innings, winning easily 13-0.

The next day we started a crucial series against the Los Angeles Dodgers, beginning with a double-header. In the first game Jeff Francis struck out ten and carried a shutout into the seventh inning; we won 3-1. In the second game Helton homered with two strikes and two outs to win the game 9-8. Todd Helton is not known for his emotional outbursts, but as he approached home plate, he let loose and did a superman dive into the pile of gathered teammates. Everyone was getting excited.

The next day Brad Hawpe homered for us off Jonathan Broxton in the eighth inning for another victory, 6-5. In the final game of the series against the Dodgers, both Matt Holliday and Troy Tulowitzki homered, and we won 9-4.

The season was wrapping up quickly. We were still behind in the standings but definitely not out of it. According to many sportscasters, we were hanging around enough to make things interesting. But most of them had already concluded that our season was finished with too big a mountain to climb. We didn't agree. "How are we going to win today?" was the question everyone asked in the clubhouse. We were committed to fighting through the final out of the season.

We traveled to San Diego and then to Los Angeles for a three-game series in each city. We swept both series and had now won eleven consecutive games. We eliminated the Dodgers from post-season play and were battling San Diego for the wild card position.

After LA, we traveled home to take on the division-leading Arizona Diamondbacks, afraid that if we lost another game we would be eliminated from the playoffs. While we were playing Arizona, San Diego was playing Milwaukee, and we knew they had a good chance of winning every game there.

Our hearts and spirits almost broke when Arizona won the first game 4-2 and clinched the division title. We still had a chance at the wild card, depending on the outcome of the final two games of the season. We beat Arizona in the second game and went into the clubhouse to watch the San Diego and Milwaukee game. San Diego closer Trevor Hoffman, one of the best relievers in the game, blew a sure-save opportunity, and Milwaukee won the game. We celebrated. *We're still alive. One game left.*

We won the last game of the season against the Diamondback's sixth starter. They were already preparing for post-season play. While we watched from the clubhouse, the stadium put the San Diego and Milwaukee game on the big screen. Securing the wild card spot was now out of our hands. We did what we needed to do. We needed a miracle. Milwaukee accomplished what we initially thought was impossible, beating San Diego the last two games. We were now tied with San Diego and would play a one-game playoff to determine the winner of the Wild Card.

On the first of October San Diego traveled to Coors Field for a winner-takes-all game. We had won home field advantage by a coin toss earlier in the month and now jumped out to an early 3-0 lead, heading into the third inning. In the top of the third Adrian Gonzalez hit his first career grand slam, giving San Diego the lead. They scored another run to go ahead by two runs going into the bottom of the third. In the second half of the inning, Todd Helton homered, cutting the lead to one run. We scored one run in the fifth inning and another in the sixth to regain the lead 6-5. I pitched in the top of the sixth inning, inheriting one runner with one out, and got Brian Giles to pop out to our shortstop. My work was done for the night. In the eighth inning we brought in closer Brian Fuentes, but the Padres tied up the game again when Brian Giles doubled and Geoff Blum scored. The game remained tied until the thirteenth inning.

In the top of the that inning, more than four hours after the game started, Scott Hairston hit a two-run homer, giving the Padres the lead 8-6. Trevor Hoffman entered the game in the bottom of the thirteenth. Hoffman is the all-time MLB saves leader, with six hundred one career saves. He knows pressure, and he knows how to close a game. We knew we were down to our last slim chance.

Matsui doubled off Hoffman to start us off, and Tulowitzki followed him with a double of his own, cutting the lead to one run. Holliday tied the game on a triple and stood only ninety feet away from a victory.

Hoffman walked Helton intentionally, bringing Jamey Carroll to the plate with nobody out. Jamey hit a fly ball to right field. Holliday tagged up, trying to score.

It was a bang-bang play at the plate. Padres catcher Michael Barrett attempted to block the plate from Holliday's slide while catching the ball on a throw from Brian Giles. Holliday beat the throw to the plate with a head-first slide, colliding with Barrett's knee and passing out after touching home. The ball bounced away from Barrett, and Holliday was called safe. The stadium erupted. Several sportswriters later commented that Barrett had successfully blocked the plate, but both the Padres manager and the first-base umpire agreed with the safe call. We were officially headed to the post season.

Two days later, on October 3, we were in Philadelphia at the official start of the post season. Our streak continued as we swept the Phillies in three games. I made my post-season debut in the sixth inning of the second game of the series. I struck out two players after surrendering a home run to slugger Ryan Howard.

We traveled to Arizona to take on the Diamondbacks once again. I entered the first game in the bottom of the seventh inning. We were leading 5-1, but the bases were loaded with two outs, and Stephen Drew stepped up to the plate. I got Drew to fly-out to right field, and we won the game by the same score. I also pitched the third game of the series, retiring all three batters I faced. We had swept the Diamondbacks in a best-of-seven series. Out of our last twenty-two games, we had won twenty-one. It was incredible. We were headed to the World Series.

Then we waited.

Cleveland and Boston were playing to determine which of them would face us in the World Series. Cleveland was leading the series 3-1, but they ended up losing three straight games to Boston. We had to wait eight days between games. This waiting period turned out to be disastrous. We began cooling off.

It is an amazing feeling to simply get to the World Series. It is an even greater experience to *play* in the World Series. We lost the first two games to Boston at historic Fenway Park. Returning to Colorado, I was called in to pitch the sixth inning to the top of the Boston line-up. Jacoby Ellsbury grounded out to our third baseman. Dustin Pedroia hit a pop-up to centerfield. And then, there I was facing David Ortiz. With fifty thousand people screaming and yelling, I could feel the mound vibrating. I threw him curveball after curveball, and he worked the count to two balls and two strikes. Then I threw a fastball past him, and he struck out swinging. As I left the field, he looked at me and smiled. The expression on his face seemed to say, *You've got to be kiddin' me.*

I pitched in every game of the World Series, but Boston silenced our bats and swept us to end the season. It was a great run of baseball, unlike anything I've ever seen, let alone be a part of.

After the World Series I became a free agent again. I turned down an offer from Houston, thinking that Colorado would extend a multi-year deal to me. Cincinnati contacted me, and I called the general manager of the Rockies and asked him to match it. I told him that I would stay if he simply matched their offer. He didn't. I was disappointed; I didn't really want to leave Colorado.

Cincinnati, here I come.

TEN

CINCINNATI LOWS

One thing that is easy to see in Scripture is that people are far from perfect. Following Jesus is a messy journey filled with mistakes as we open ourselves to the forgiveness, counsel, and guidance of the Spirit.

BASEBALL, just like any game worth playing or career worth pursuing, is full of ups and downs. I experienced many lows in Kansas City, battling through injuries and bouncing back and forth between starting and pitching from the bullpen. Losing one hundred games in a season—*sixty percent of the games*—is a major frustration and trial for any athlete. When we are surrounded by an atmosphere of failure, constantly dwelling on the negative, it's easy to become trapped in a cycle of despair and gloom. Negativity hinders success.

Thanks to "The Streak" I experienced with the Colorado Rockies, I got my first taste of the post season—and all the way to the World Series at that. Playing that magical season in Colorado was like a kiss from heaven. In less than two years I had gone from the valleys to the mountaintops—figuratively and literally.

During the off-season I received many invitations to speak at churches, schools, and all kinds of venues, mainly due to having pitched in the World Series. I challenged kids to dream big and to believe that their dreams were significant. I shared stories about baseball and some of the leadership lessons I had learned. It was during this time that I became passionate about public speaking. However, I also got to experience some of the frustrations that can occur when you are trying to walk intimately with Jesus Christ.

Jesus once said that people will recognize His followers by their love for one another. In His life, death, and resurrection, Jesus fulfilled all the laws and demands of the old covenant and gave us a new covenant to live out—love God and love your neighbor. But it seems that many Christians are filled more with fear and fight than with the radical love of our Savior Jesus Christ.

We are fearful of what others may think of us, so we tend to structure our churches more like professional organizations or country clubs than places of hospitality for all—yes, even those who aren't like us or the marginalized and the poor. Too often we create church cultures filled with people who say they want to follow in the way of Jesus Christ but in reality turn their backs on those who appear to be different, basing their superficial judgments on clothes, piercings, tattoos, socioeconomic distinctions, skin color, political beliefs—the list goes on and on. We judge those who are different and expect our fear-based, guilt-inducing judgment to bring change that can be accomplished only by the Spirit of God. We retreat to churches that are homogenous houses of safety where everyone looks and thinks alike.

One of my friends was in a Christian bookstore recently. He was interested in purchasing *Jesus Manifesto*, by Len Sweet and Frank Viola, a book that focuses on the centrality of Christ in our daily lives. As he was looking at the cover and thumbing through the chapters, one of the salespeople approached him and said, "You really need to be careful with that book. Those authors are really dangerous. They support house churches and really suspect theology." *This is how Christians talk about one another?* My friend told me that salesperson couldn't have been more than twenty years old, and he felt sad that he was living with so much fear. My friend wondered, *Doesn't he know that the love of the one who lives in us drives away fear?*

Christians in our culture sometimes seem to be too comfortable with negativity and judgmental attitudes. We fight over styles of worship and doctrinal interpretations. We declare that those who have a different opinion on scriptural issues than we do must be "heretics." We fight over what day to worship God, what is appropriate to wear to worship, and how God prefers to be addressed in prayer.

We fight because we want to be right. We launch attacks on other Christians because we want other people to follow God and believe in God the same way we do. Instead of trusting in the Holy Spirit, we try to "play God," solving everyone's problems to the best of our ability, forming others to be like us instead of allowing God to transform them into the image of our Lord Jesus Christ.

One thing that is easy to see in Scripture is that people are far from perfect. Following Jesus is a messy journey filled with mistakes as we open ourselves to the forgiveness, counsel, and guidance of the Spirit. It is not based on a formula; it is a dynamic and mysterious way of life. Jesus said that He alone is the way, the truth, and the life. That means that we learn what it means to follow Jesus as we live. Truth is not a proposition to which we give mental assent; truth is a person we know, trust, and love. Truth is found in relationship with the person of Jesus Christ.

The essential confession in the Scriptures is this: *Jesus Christ is Lord.* Why can't we followers of Jesus come together around our confession? We don't have to agree with everything our brothers and sisters believe, but we do have to love each other. We are so afraid of agreeing to disagree on issues that are often nonessentials of faith that we simply choose not to be friends if we don't see eye to eye. *Jesus Christ is Lord*—this is what matters. This is the starting place. The family blood runs deeper than our disagreements when we live by this simple yet profound confession.

I've had teammates confess to me about not going to church or to chapel. They felt the need to defend themselves to me, even though I never judged them. One of my dearest friends shared his story with me about going to church with a girl he was dating, and she ended up telling him that he had to walk in front of everyone at the church and proclaim his faith or else she didn't think he was a Christian. That is not what it means to be a church.

That is not what it means to be a Christian. That is sheer guilt manipulation and has no place in the life of following Jesus. We must be very careful not to make anyone our "project" or an "item on our agenda." God calls us to love people and be, *really be*, with them and for them.

God can do as He chooses. He has used pillars of fire and pillars of salt. He has used talking donkeys and burning bushes and fish and bread. God has used kings and queens, fishermen and prostitutes, and even a few religious leaders. The question for us is this: *Do we believe that the Spirit can and will work over the course of someone's life?* Too often we force the issue instead of trusting in the sufficiency and sovereignty of God to work in someone's life.

Cincinnati Reds—2008

Playing baseball for a living is a serendipitous journey of inequality. At the time of this writing, with Jim Thome knocking at the door with five hundred eighty-nine homers, Ken Griffey Jr., one of the best hitters of all time, is one of only seven players in the six-hundred-home-run club. He has played twenty-one seasons in the majors and never once made it to the World Series. I had played only six seasons and already been to the World Series. But Griffey made just a little bit more money than I did. Now we were teammates, playing for the Cincinnati Reds.

I signed with Cincinnati on January 22. When I arrived for spring training, the very first thing I was told was that they would like me to be a starting pitcher again. *You have got to be kidding me!* However, after two weeks of trying in spring training, they moved me to the bullpen for good. I struggled to find my role and my place on the team. I entered some games in the third inning, and in other games I pitched in the ninth—if it wasn't a save situation. *I couldn't believe this was happening again.*

About halfway through the season I approached my manager, Dusty Baker. Dusty is a good manager who has been around baseball for a long time. I asked him what my role was and told him that I needed to know my role to stay focused and sharp and to know what to expect when I headed to the ballpark.

Dusty pulled out a piece of paper. On it was written "Short-relief, long-relief, set-up, game finisher without a save."

"Dusty, that's not *a* role—that's *every* role in the bullpen. How am I supposed to prepare for that?"

"Jeremy, you can do all these things. I know what I'm doing."

We got into a little bit of an argument, and I finally walked away before I became angry. At first I was so frustrated; it reminded me of my experiences in Kansas City. But then I decided to trust. I remember whispering a simple prayer: *God, I'm choosing to trust you on this one.*

At the end of the season I had seventy-four appearances with seventy-eight innings pitched. I made the three hundredth appearance of my career on May 2 against the Braves in a losing effort. I was one of only five pitchers in the National League to pitch seventy-five innings and average one strikeout per inning. I had one win, one loss, five holds, and a 3.33 ERA. With a decent year in a small ballpark, I found myself at the end of the season—once again a free agent. I knew that it would be almost impossible to get a setup job with another team with only five holds.

Dusty came up to me at the end of the year and said, "I know you didn't like how I used you, but I'd love to have you back." As a team, we finished fourth in our division. One of the highlights of the year was watching Griffey hit his sixth hundredth home run against the Florida Marlins in early June.

I prayed hard. I asked God to help me find a team on the West Coast where I could be close to home, where I could be with my family. I prayed fervently for a two-year deal. It wasn't long before the San Francisco Giants called.

I received a call from my agent. He knew my prayers and the desires of my heart. He told me that San Francisco was really interested in me. They were looking for a veteran who could throw strikes, get outs, and bring some leadership to the bullpen. He told me that the Giants had a solid closer in Brian Wilson, and they wanted someone who could help put the ball in his hands. San Francisco had called twice and was very serious about pursuing me.

One year earlier San Francisco called me after I played in the World Series with Colorado. At that time they extended me a two-year deal for very low pay. I had told my agent to tell them never to call me again. What they had offered me the year before was an insult.

My agent and Giants management continued to dialogue. The Giants knew I had held out almost all the way to spring training before signing with Cincinnati. They asked my agent, "Is he going to hold out again this year, or is he willing to make a quick negotiation?"

With great wisdom my agent replied, "If you offer him what he's worth, he'll sign."

A few weeks passed. San Francisco contacted my agent at midnight and said, "We'll have a contract ready for Jeremy in the morning."

Without knowing about San Francisco's latest communication, I had gotten up early the next morning to go hunting. My agent texted me while I was dragging a deer down the side of a mountain. One of the reasons I like to go hunting is that no one can get in touch with me, my cell phone doesn't get reception in my regular hunting grounds, and it's a place I can go to be left alone to converse with God and think. Somehow, at this particular moment, I had cell service. The text simply said, "Call me immediately."

I ran to my truck—where I had no cell service—and drove down the mountain until I reached a place I could get the call through to my agent. He said, "San Francisco is on the line with me, and they need a decision. There's someone else they want to extend the offer to if you don't take it. Jeremy, they are offering everything that you've prayed about."

I asked for five minutes to call my wife.

I called Larisa and told her what was happening. She asked if I wanted to play in San Francisco. I told her that they were giving me everything we had prayed for.

But—and I hate to admit this—I was sinfully homophobic. I really disliked being around homosexuals. It was a fear based on ignorance and judgment. Every time I had played in San Francisco in the past, I spent the entire time in my hotel room until it was time to go to the ballpark.

When I went to Cincinnati to play for the Reds, one of the baristas at the coffee shop I frequented was openly and unabashedly gay. At first I didn't even want to acknowledge the guy, and I even tried not to order from him. My son accompanied me on many of my trips, and the barista would talk to my son, entertain my son, and slowly something happened to me. I started to see this man as a person, a human being, and not a "category."

It is so easy because of our sinfulness to label and dehumanize people, and when we have allowed ourselves to get to that place, it becomes even easier to dismiss them. But something happened. I started feeling true compassion toward this young man.

And then it hit me, *This guy experiences judgment and condemnation all the time. He is a human being. He has feelings and dreams and hopes. I don't want to be the guy who judges him and ignores him. I can't imagine the pain he's in because of people like me.* This experience also reminded me of how far from following the example of Jesus Christ and His interaction with people His own culture had marginalized that some Christians in our culture have drifted.

I started seeking him out whenever I went to Starbucks. I began having extended conversations, and I really enjoyed talking to him and seeking to understand. I came to value the conversations, and my son liked him too. This barista helped soften my heart and helped me go to a place where God would forever change my life.

I called my agent back and said, "We'll take it." God had answered my prayers. Little did I know my journey with Jesus Christ would go in directions I would never have dreamed.

ELEVEN

STRIKING OUT INJUSTICE

I USED TO LIVE IN SUCH A WAY THAT I TURNED MY BACK ON THOSE WHO WERE SUFFERING, THOSE WHO WERE DIFFERENT THAN ME. NOW I SEE THEM AND I HAVE TO DO *SOMETHING.*

I NEVER THOUGHT about justice, poverty, or other social issues when I was growing up. I once saw a homeless person and told him, "Get a job. You're lazy. Take a shower and cut off your beard. Go to McDonald's and be a janitor. Do something, man." I rolled my eyes and walked away. I didn't have a compassionate bone in my body—not for the kid who was getting bullied, not for the orphan in Africa, not for anyone.

I heard some talk about abortion growing up, but it was usually discussed in one-dimensional terms. Had it been addressed from a biblical perspective, we would have been talking about adopting unwanted babies and providing care for unwed mothers. Instead, we talked about abortion from the perspective of a conservative political agenda that created a lot of division.

On one occasion, I went to a homeless shelter to help serve meals the residents. I don't think I really even saw them as people—as human beings. I was too self-centered to really care. I thought the shelter was dirty and the residents smelled funny. I had no desire to talk to them or hang out with them. I just wanted to leave.

I now know that those faces covered in the dirt and grime of the daily grind have incredible stories to share. Some of them are tortured by addictions and mental struggles. Some of them have lived on the streets for so long that they can't imagine life any other way. In the book *Same Kind of Different as Me*, two worlds collide when a

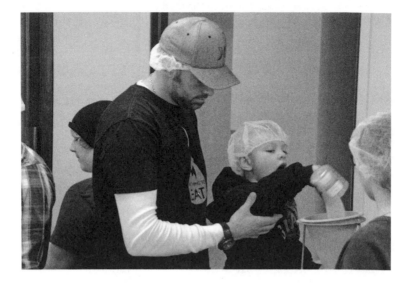

white international art dealer and a Black homeless man become friends. It's a beautiful picture of what's possible when people are willing look at each other through eyes of compassion, choosing to look past the masks we wear.

When I played for the Royals, Mike Sweeney helped me get a glimpse of the incredible need around me. He invited me to help him with "Lunch for Life," raising money for crisis pregnancy centers in the Kansas City area. For the first time, I really saw what a difference we could make as professional athletes. God used Mike on numerous other occasions in my life. He helped teach me that doing works of justice for others is imperative for Christ followers.

My next awakening came when I played for the Rockies. In the summer Denver is a community of homeless teenagers. I was headed to Starbucks as part of my game-day routine and saw a young teenage girl sitting outside with a black eye and a bloody lip. For some reason, the thought entered my mind that she had been raped the night before, and I knew I had to do something.

I asked if she was hungry, if she wanted something to eat. She nodded hopefully. I went into Starbucks and bought several items so she would have something to eat. We had a conversation—human being to human being— both created in God's image, both broken, and both desperately needing restoration and redemption. When we finished talking, she smiled and walked away.

And then, when I moved to San Francisco, my life took a whole new trajectory.

As noted earlier, Dave Batstone educated me on the horrors of human trafficking, a hidden evil with a very powerful presence in our daily lives. We unknowingly help to fund slavery by the things we buy and the ways we choose to spend our money. When I buy certain types of chocolate at the checkout line, I'm helping to fund slavery, specifically the children who work in the cocoa fields of the Ivory Coast. The West African country of Ivory Coast is the world's largest producer of cocoa, with more than forty percent of the world's production. You can get more information on cocoa production at <www.the darksideofchocolate.org>. Major chocolate producers knowingly use this source and could choose to end this form of slavery by raising their prices by a mere dime.

Most people would willingly pay a dime more if they really knew what was happening to child laborers in Africa.

A friend gave me the video *The Dark Side of Chocolate,* which shares the stories of children who are forced to work in the cocoa industry, never getting paid. One boy shared a story about sleeping in the fields at night, and he has never tasted chocolate, something to which many Americans jokingly admit being addicted. A reporter asked him what he would say to those who are eating the fruits of his labor. The boy replied, "I wouldn't have anything nice to say to them. I'd tell them that they are eating my flesh."

We help to fund slavery when we purchase clothes made in sweatshops that have no integrity plan to lift workers out of extreme poverty. American clothing companies outsource their labor to other countries, saving millions of dollars and increasing the profits for the company and its shareholders. The countries often do not have the labor laws that we do, employing women and children who work ridiculous hours in horrid conditions for very low pay. In the end, we consumers save a couple of bucks on a shirt or a pair of jeans because the sweat and blood of someone else produced the article of clothing.

In His first sermon, Jesus proclaimed that He came to set slaves free and release the oppressed (see Luke 4:18). Those who follow Jesus are compelled to do the same things. Isaiah, the inspiration for Jesus' sermon, also said this:

> Is not this the kind of fasting I have chosen: to loose the chains of injustice and untie the cords of the yoke, to set the oppressed free and break every yoke? Is it not to share your food with the hungry and to provide the poor wanderer with shelter—whcn you see the naked, to clothe them, and not to turn away from your own flesh and blood? Then your light will break forth like the dawn, and your healing will quickly appear; then your righteousness will go before you, and the glory of the LORD will be your rear guard (*Isaiah 58:6-8*).

I once saw a prostitute walking the streets of San Francisco, and my heart broke. I am convinced that she has not freely chosen this as a way of life. Her life and her dreams have been stolen from her. In major cities, many prostitutes have been brought over from other countries. They don't know English, and they have been told the police will throw them into prison if they try to escape. They are deceived by the lies of their captors, who take away their visas and ship them around the country, never giving them a dime of the money they earn.

Matt Cain is one of those guys who is more than a teammate—he is a brother to me. One day in chapel we were talking about generosity and giving. He asked me what Larisa and I do to make a difference with our financial resources. He was surprised when I shared with him what we do and why we do it. I told him honestly that the money isn't really ours in the first place. All our resources belong to God. We are stewards of what we have and should use what we have for God's glory. I give cheerfully to people and causes that proclaim the love of Christ by doing justice work. Matt responded by declaring to me that he wanted to join me in a project. Together we helped build orphanages in Gulu, Uganda. This is part of what it means to love your neighbor as yourself. I like having a place I can call home; now these children have a place they can call home too.

Do you think someone has the time to think about Jesus when he or she is just trying to figure out how to survive until tomorrow? When we provide something to eat for the hungry, when we build orphanages for the orphans, when we dig clean water wells for the thirsty, when we set the slaves free, we do it because we love Jesus and love people. Maybe they will see the love of Jesus because they see it in us. But even if they don't, we serve them anyway, because Christ calls us to do these things. The kingdom of God is breaking in when these things happen. The Good News of Jesus Christ is delivered through our acts of justice for the poor and the marginalized. It is the responsibility of the Church to live out this message among all nations.

I used to live in such a way that I turned my back on those who were suffering, those who were different than me. Now I see them and I have to do *something*. As God continues to reveal himself to me, I'm learning that the gospel isn't something you just believe in—the gospel is a way you live.

One of the coolest things I've done recently was hang out at a teenage homeless shelter in San Francisco. I visited with the kids, and they told me about the programs they participate in, how they are getting educations as well as having a stable and consistent source of food. I asked one of the directors, "Why are all these kids on the streets? Where are their families? Why do they run away?" The answer was crushing; almost all of these kids have been trafficked, some even by their own families. The kids don't know where to go or who to trust. They don't have a home or anyone to protect them.

Thanks to this shelter, these "street kids" get their GEDs and are given the opportunity through City College in downtown San Francisco to get a college education. Their lives are changing. New dreams are being born inside them. Hope is restored where despair once reigned.

The directors asked me if I would be willing to speak at one of their graduations. I was honored. It was held at a local church, and there were thirty graduates.

One of the kids sang an amazing song that touched the hearts of everyone there. I told the kids that I was proud of them, that I was humbled and impressed by their fortitude and perseverance. I said, "You have been failed by those who should have protected and loved you. But you have not given up. You have pressed on, determined to do something with your lives. You are all living miracles." I wanted and tried to encourage them, but they encouraged me more than I could ever encourage them.

I was so inspired by these kids.

San Francisco—2009

Almost immediately I began having a breakout career year with the Giants. I started off the season with a twenty-eight-inning scoreless streak that didn't end until after the All-Star Break, on July 28. I finished the season with an ERA of 1.73 and pitched in a major-league-leading seventy-four games. I had thirty-three holds, which was only two away from the record, and at the end of the year I was awarded the This Year in Baseball's Setup Man of the Year Award.

I pitched with passion, knowing that I wasn't just playing for myself but was playing to make a difference in the world. The mound became a place of worship for me. I talked with God—a running conversation—intentionally praising Him and intensely focusing on the task at hand. I do not take for granted the gifts God has given to me. I desperately want to honor God with every aspect of my life, including baseball.

At the end of the season I was nominated for the Jefferson Award for Public Service and the Hutchinson Award. It is a tremendous honor just to be nominated for these awards. It was the things I did to serve God that led to these nominations.

There had been a time when I thought my best service to God was telling people, including teammates, how lost they were. This approach does not work. I had lots of long conversations with my friend Mike King, who encouraged me to embrace a broader perspective on what it means to bear witness to the good news of Jesus. He encouraged me to be a blessing to my teammates, to draw attention to the glimpses of the image of God that shows through in their lives, regardless of whether or not they are aware of it. We talked about living a life that emitted the fragrance of Christ, about how people are really tired of Christians who come across as judgmental and self-righteous. I remember Mike saying, "Jeremy, if you focus on cooperating with God's mission of restoration—serving the poor and marginalized, proclaiming the Good News that is really good news for all, and blessing those around you—people around you will want to know what you think about Jesus instead of trying to avoid you." He was right.

My life with God was becoming richer and deeper. Professionally, as a baseball player, I couldn't begin to imagine the adventure that would unfold in my second year with the Giants.

TWELVE

I STARTED PRAYING HARD, SEEKING GOD, AND
THINKING ABOUT MY JUDGMENTAL ATTITUDE
TOWARD OTHERS. I RECEIVED A CLEAR SENSE
FROM THE HOLY SPIRIT THAT I NEEDED TO
HUMBLE MYSELF AND BEGIN PRAYING FOR
AND BLESSING MY FELLOW TEAMMATES.

MR. NEUKOM, the owner of the San Francisco Giants, is a phenomenal owner and a very smart businessman. He has a long-term plan for helping the Giants stay competitive, and part of that plan was offering extensions to the current pitching staff. After the breakout year I had in 2009, the Giants extended my contract through 2011 with an option for 2012.

The very first thing I did after signing the extension was to go into his office, shake his hand, and thank him. Mr. Neukom is a justice guy too, making sure that the poor have lawyers and helping those who are struggling. I wanted him to know that his money wasn't going to be used to live a lavish lifestyle but to help make a difference around the world.

After I signed the contract extension, the assistant general manager, Bobby Evans, contacted me and said that a mistake had been made. For the management it was a very costly mistake—they accidentally added *half a million dollars* to my contract. Technically, it was a signed deal, even though Bobby acknowledged that it was just a typo. Somebody accidentally hit the "5" key, and as a result I would be receiving a half million dollars more based on my contract. There was nothing management could do, because it was a legal and binding contract.

I didn't even have to think about it. "Bobby, I'm going to give you back that money," I said.

"Jeremy, you know you don't have to do that. This is a signed legal contract, and we're obligated to pay you the amount written in the contract."

"I realize I don't *have* to give it back. But as a believer in Jesus, I have no choice but to give it back. Even though it may seem hard to understand, it's the right thing for me to do."

I gave the money back. The contract was rewritten, and I signed a new one. I know I did the right thing. One day someone's going to be reminded of this story, and I'll be able to say that I acted with integrity, that it was part of my baseball legacy.

I left Spokane for spring training, driving with a friend. Not long into the trip, we saw a car struggling in the treacherous, icy conditions. My friend and I quickly pulled over to the shoulder to provide space for it to pass us. Suddenly an oncoming car lost all control when it hit black ice and headed straight for us. The collision was shocking, and the vehicle smashed clear up to the windshield of my car. I glanced over at my friend in the passenger seat. It was a miracle we were still alive and conscious. The wreck registered with the computer in my vehicle, and I later learned that the other driver was going fifty-five miles per hour when it hit us.

The frame of my car bent significantly under the impact, and my friend and I had to kick our doors multiple times to get out of the car. There were other cars still sliding by us, and we knew we had to get out as soon as we could. During my struggle to kick open the car door, fueled by adrenaline coursing through my body, I could tell that I was not injured. The airbag had caught me squarely, and other than a little whiplash, nothing was broken. I whispered, *Thank you, God.*

I ran over to check on the other driver. She had been thrown from the driver's seat and was hanging out the rear window. At first I thought she was dead, but thankfully, she survived too. After surveying the damage, a sheriff approached me and said, "I don't know what you believe or who you believe in, but you better keep believing. As hard as she hit you, you should be dead."

Larisa, my pregnant wife, and our son were supposed to be traveling with me. At the last minute, she and I decided it would be better for them to fly to spring training a couple days after I got things set up in Scottsdale, Arizona. The whole experience put so many things into perspective for me about what's really important in life.

Spring training got underway. Every spring training begins with new hopes for a perfect season, and this year was even more so for me, since I had just escaped death. During the off-season, I inadvertently left my glove in San Francisco. Mr. Neukom, who at the time was the managing owner of the Giants, was walking through the clubhouse and saw my glove lying there, picked it up, and brought it with him to Scottsdale. Arriving at our sports complex, he walked on to the field to personally hand-deliver the glove to me while I was gathered with other players in a circle stretching out. Some of the younger guys on the team were freaked out when they saw the owner walking onto the field.

Mr. Neukom looked at me and said, "Well, Jeremy, I guess I'm your caddy now, bringing your glove to you on the field."

Mr. Neukom is classy but approachable, so I responded to his joke by saying, "Yeah, tell you what. How about you take it and put it in my locker, on the left side?" *And he did it!* My teammates were shocked. Matt Cain gave me such a hard time for treating the owner like that. I called Mizuno and ordered a glove for Mr. Neukom as a thank you for the good humor.

The season started well, even though I was still recovering from the car wreck. I picked up a save against the Atlanta Braves but was up and down for the first half of the season. Hoping to duplicate the amazing year of 2009, I ended up struggling instead. I pitched regularly, but it wasn't quite up to my standards. By mid-season, I was coming into form, earning a hold and a save in back-to-back games against the Dodgers. We went to Arizona to play the Diamondbacks. I was warming up to come into the game when all of a sudden I felt an explosion of pain on my left side. *No way. Not now. Please, not now.* I knew this was not good.

Immediately I stopped throwing. I walked from the bullpen and went straight to the clubhouse. Manager Bruce Bochy was informed that I was no longer available to come into the game. After the game he asked me what was wrong. "I can't breathe, I can't move, I can't sit. I have no idea what's wrong." The team doctor started feeling around and noticed that the pain was located on the left side of my body, in the oblique-area, right on the ribcage.

The next morning I went to the doctor to get an MRI. He glanced at the results. All I heard was "Oh." *That can't be good.* He showed me the MRI—a seven-centimeter tear in my left oblique. When I was with the Royals I was out for six weeks with a three-centimeter tear in my right oblique. This time it tore from front to back, which was highly unusual, and it was torn completely off the bottom rib. I couldn't sneeze, cough, breathe, or laugh without intense pain.

There was some good news, however. The location of the tear was in a stabilizing oblique, not a power oblique. The team doctor said I could start throwing again as soon as the pain went away, and within two weeks I was throwing again.

The Giants placed me on the disabled list on July 24, and I came off it on August 18. I was brought back early since we were low on bullpen help and were playing the Phillies and St. Louis. My first outing was pretty rough, which usually happens when you come back from the disabled list. I spent the remainder of the season fighting to get back my role on the team. For the last three weeks of September I pitched about once a week, and I was beginning to get really frustrated from being overlooked.

We started the month of July seven games behind the Padres in the division standings but had a solid month nonetheless. By the end of September we had finally taken the division lead. We entered the final series of the season against the Padres, needing only one win to secure the division title.

The Padres won the first two games.

Once again, it came down to the final game of the season. We used six pitchers in the game, and they all pitched brilliantly, resulting in a four-hit shutout victory. We were headed to post-season play.

For the league division series we faced the Atlanta Braves. Every game was decided by one run. I was thrilled that we won the series three games to one. I was not thrilled that I didn't pitch in a single game during that series. In fact, I had hardly pitched at all during the last two weeks of September. I was frustrated and discouraged. I told Larisa and a few friends and family members how hard it was to stay focused because I just didn't understand why I wasn't pitching. My father-in-law caught me off guard when he said, "You need to pray through some of the judgments you've been making."

I knew that Scripture said, "Do not judge, and you will not be judged" (Luke 6:37). At first I didn't think I was being judgmental. But the more I thought about it, the clearer it became. Forgiveness is impossible as long as we are judging others; as long as there is judgment, things will not change. You do not quickly forgive those you judge.

I started praying hard, seeking God, and thinking about my judgmental attitude toward others. I received a clear sense from the Holy Spirit that I needed to humble myself and begin praying for and blessing my fellow teammates. I knew I needed to be as concerned about being faithful to Jesus and an encouragement to my teammates as I was about my personal worries over my pitching status.

I started praying, but things didn't change immediately. I was still struggling with the frustration I felt toward my manager and coaches and really wanted to pitch and contribute to my team's success. I believed I could make a difference with my pitching. One day while walking around the outfield before a game, I was thinking, praying, and getting angry and worked up again about my situation. I sat down in the middle of right field and said, *God, speak to me. I'm listening. Reveal to me where I've judged people unfairly.* I started going over the names of all my teammates. Nothing happened. No names came to mind—just silence. Then an idea popped into my head. I walked to every position on the field, and at each position I thought about my specific teammates who played those positions.

I was devastated. God began to reveal to me that I had judged each and every one of my teammates throughout the course of the season. It broke my heart to see ways I had misrepresented Jesus to my friends, my teammates. But this experience opened the door to forgiveness and change. I walked back into the clubhouse and remember seeing my teammates through new eyes, deeply enjoying each and every one of them.

I still desperately wanted to pitch, but this experience—my prayers and my resulting new awareness of my sinfulness—was changing me. I learned to listen deeply. Whenever the media or other players spoke negatively about one of my teammates, I began praying for him and looked for ways to encourage and bless him. I felt called to pray for every one of my teammates, although I didn't tell them what I was doing or why I was doing it. I just wanted to break the vicious cycle of judgment that comes with this game we play for a living.

We traveled to Philadelphia to meet the Phillies for the National League Championship Series. The Phillies had signed my dear friend Mike Sweeney in the middle of the season when Ryan Howard was injured. It was Sweeney's first experience with post-season play. He got one at bat against the Reds in the series and singled. Awesome! Mike had a batting average of 1.000 in the post-season.

We won the first game against the Phillies by one run. I finally made a post-season appearance in game two. We were losing 3-1 when I came in with runners on first and second and one out. Ryan Howard was at the plate. I struck out Howard, but the runners advanced on a double steal. I intentionally walked Jayson Werth, and my night was done. All three runners ended up scoring on a double, and we lost the game 6-1.

The series returned to San Francisco, and we won the next two games, taking a 3-1 lead in the best-of-seven series. In game five, with two outs and two runners on base, we were down by two runs in the top of the ninth, and I got called in to pitch to Shane Victorino. I struck him out, but we still lost the game. We traveled back to Philadelphia for game six.

Throughout the series I continued praying, slowly learning that prayer was more important than pitching. I prayed for my teammates by name. I prayed that God would use my current situation to shape me more deeply to be the man God created me to be. I confessed to God that I would trust whatever happened. Even though I knew that a "woe-is-me pity party" was always waiting close by, enticing me to give into despair, I prayed that God would let me dwell in gratitude and thankfulness for all the things I had been blessed with. I prayed that I would be prepared for whatever opportunities came my way and that I would continue to worship Jesus even if an opportunity didn't happen. I decided to trust God instead of judging my manager, Bochy, or anyone else.

It's hard enough to beat Philadelphia. It's harder to beat Philadelphia in Philadelphia. And we all knew that if we had to go to a seventh game, Philly would be tough to beat. In our minds, game six was our most opportune chance.

Jonathan Sanchez started, and the Phillies jumped out to a quick lead, scoring two in the bottom of the first. We tied the game in the top of the third, and then Sanchez started struggling in the bottom half of the inning.

Placido Polanco walked to start the inning. The phone in the bullpen rang, and Ramon Ramirez and I were instructed to start warming up. It was so unusual for me to warm up this early in a game. *What in the world are you up to, God? What have you got planned?* I really didn't think putting me in the game in the third inning was the best way to use me. Then Chase Utley was hit by a pitch to put two runners on with no one out.

All chaos broke out.

Utley and Sanchez started yelling at each other. Sometime the previous year, Sanchez threw a ball too close to Utley's head, and Utley remembered it. No one really knows if it was intentional or not. The two kept yelling at each other, and the benches cleared. *And then the bullpens cleared.* I had thrown only about five or six warm-up pitches when *everyone* spilled out onto the field to join the skirmish.

Part of being a team means joining the brawls on the field. Instinctively, I started to run onto the field when bullpen coach Mark Gardner grabbed me and said, "You stay here. You warm up." I stayed in the bullpen, even though the fans were giving me a hard time and questioning my manhood. Because of what was happening on the field, I was able to get fifteen more warm-up throws in; my adrenaline was pumping, and everything felt great. As soon as the scuttle settled, I was called in to the game.

Two runners on base.

Game tied.

No outs.

National League Championship Series.

Millions of people watching all over the world.

Ryan Howard at the plate.

Yes, I thought about the fact that Ryan Howard was the first player I had ever faced in my first post-season appearance with the Colorado Rockies. I knew what he was capable of, but I felt a strong confidence as I approached the mound and an incredible amount of peace. Bochy looked at me and said, "Keep this thing close, because we're gonna win it."

I took my final warm-up pitches. The stadium was throbbing with energy and expectation by the fans that this was the moment when the Phillies would take this series back. I took a deep breath, and the game resumed. I quickly got ahead of him with a curveball and a fastball inside, two quick strikes. I followed with a couple of fastballs outside to see if he would chase them. He didn't. With the count 2-2, I threw a fastball high and struck him out.

One out. Runners still on first and second. I was determined to keep them from scoring.

Jayson Werth stepped up to the plate. Jayson had hit me pretty well in the past. We battled. He finally hit a fly ball to right field for the second out.

Come on, Jeremy—take another deep breath. Two down, one to go, just one more batter to take care of. I was engaged in a very active conversation with myself and God the whole time. *Here we go.*

Shane Victorino stepped up to the plate, determined to come through for his team by putting them ahead in the game. Mike Sweeney had joked with me that some of the Phillies players thought I was cheating by doctoring the ball since it was moving all over the place. I laughed and told Sweeney to tell him that I was indeed cheating. Victorino took a huge swing at the second pitch and hit a corkscrew of a grounder to Aubrey Huff at first base, who stepped onto the bag to retire the side.

The bench erupted.

We went down quickly in the top of the fourth, and Bochy sent me back out to pitch the bottom of the inning. All my pitches were working like magic, a ground-out, a strikeout, and a flyout. Inning over. The Phillies' momentum was extinguished, but we were locked in an intense battle.

The game remained tied until the top of the eighth inning when Juan Uribe hit a solo home run to give us our first lead of the game. That was enough. We won the game 3-2 and the series 4-2. The Giants were playing in the World Series for the first time since 1954, when the team was located in New York. This was the first time a San Francisco-located Giants team would appear in the World Series. And I was going back to the World Series for a second time. Unbelievable!

We were celebrating in the clubhouse when Bochy addressed the media: "Hey, let's not forget what Affeldt did today, because he saved us."

When I heard that, I looked to heaven. I had been living in a pity party. I had been trapped in my own little world, and only through prayer had I been able to release that self-pity, anger, frustration—and those judgments. Through Bochy I heard God say, *Jeremy, learn to trust me. My servants are my servants for a reason. Just trust me. I have a plan that results in my glory. You need to trust my plan.*"

Cody Ross was selected as the Most Valuable Player (MVP) of the series. He said, "I might've won the award, but there was a new MVP every night." I finally felt as if I were a meaningful part of our success. Everyone on the team contributed to the wins.

After the game my dear friend Mike Sweeney, who had made such a huge contribution to helping me not only become a successful Major League Baseball player but also become a deeper follower of Jesus Christ, was sitting in the dugout watching the celebration on the field. I left the celebratory dog pile, walked over to him, and gave him a big hug. No one has more class than Mike Sweeney.

There are times my prayers sound more like screams of frustration. I know that God hears the cries of my heart and leads me—most often on a path I would never have chosen for myself. The path is often a struggle; the struggles draw me closer to my Lord. When I finally take the time to look back, I see just how good, how faithful, how amazing Jesus Christ has been to me.

World Series—Texas Rangers

Almost everyone thought Texas was going to win. As a team, the Phillies were a lot like the Rangers. We had just beat Philly; all we had to do was play the game our way, and we knew we could win. The series started in San Francisco; the whole city was hungry for a World Series victory.

The first game was supposed to be a pitcher's duel—Timmy Lincecum squaring off against Cliff Lee. With two of the best pitchers in baseball, the game turned into a hitting derby. We ended up winning a slugfest 11-7.

In the second game my good friend Matt Cain was absolutely unhittable. We exploded for seven runs in the eighth inning and won the game 9-0.

The third game was in Texas, and we fell short, losing 4-2; but we still had a one-game lead in the series.

The fourth game was played on Halloween. I remember my son Walker trick-or-treating in the hotel. Everyone was excited and trying hard to stay focused on the task at hand, not getting too far ahead of ourselves. Madison Bumgarner pitched flawlessly, allowing only three hits in eight innings, and our closer, Brian Wilson, pitched a quick ninth for the save. We won 4-0 and were only one win away from being World Series champions.

Game five was a rematch of the first game, with Tim Lincecum pitching against Cliff Lee. Both pitchers were near perfect through the first six innings, pitching shutout ball. With two outs and two runners on, Edgar Renteria blasted a home run in the top of the seventh, giving us a 3-0 lead. The Rangers were running out of outs. Nelson Cruz homered in the bottom of the seventh, cutting the lead to two runs. The eighth inning passed quickly, and soon we were only three outs away from victory.

Brian Wilson was amped and ready to face the heart of the Ranger lineup. He struck out slugger Josh Hamilton on four pitches. One down. Vladimir Guerrero grounded out on the first pitch Wilson threw. Two down. Nelson Cruz stepped up to the plate, and with a full count, Wilson struck him out. Out number three. It was one of the quickest saves Brian had all year.

World Champions!

The bullpen and dugout poured onto the field. The growing pile of players circled Brian Wilson, jumping up and down in pure, childlike ecstasy. For the first time in nearly sixty years, the San Francisco Giants were champions. Larisa and our boys celebrated with me on the field. It was an experience like nothing else, one I was glad to share with my family.

The owners rented a double-decker plane to fly us back to San Francisco. I was so drained that I fell asleep before take-off. We got back to San Francisco around 4:30 in the morning, and thousands of screaming fans welcomed us home. It was awesome.

The whole city was celebrating. It was easier to walk through town than to drive anywhere. I ate breakfast and went next door to a hair salon to get a haircut and shave. Two older ladies were sitting there, looked at me, and started crying. They were so happy that the Giants had finally won the World Series and celebrated the entire time I was getting my hair cut.

Two days after winning the World Series, we continued the celebration on a trolley parade through downtown San Francisco. Approximately two million people participated in the parade, packing the streets—even standing on the bus stops. My ears rang for hours because of the decibel level of the gathered fans. Walker joined Larisa and me on the trolley. He loved throwing out candy to the fans. Eventually the excitement wore him out, and he collapsed into a deep sleep.

I had never experienced anything like this.

Words simply cannot capture the joy and thrill of the whole experience.

THIRTEEN

GENERATION ALIVE

Approximately one in eight people lacks
access to safe drinking water. We flush
our toilets every day and don't even
think twice that the water in that
toilet is cleaner than the drinking
water in other countries.

I BELIEVE God led me to San Francisco for a reason. The purpose was so much greater than winning the Set-Up Man of the Year award and much more significant than winning the World Series. I believe God led me to San Francisco to learn more deeply about what it means to follow the Lord Jesus Christ.

For most of my life I played baseball mostly for me. I obsessed about my statistics and constantly worried about securing my role and position on the team. There was a selfish, immature part of me that was easily frustrated when things didn't go my way. But when I came to San Francisco, I was truly on a journey to discover a deeper, more robust meaning of what it means to be a person who embraces a broader definition of the gospel, the good news of Jesus Christ.

As mentioned previously, shortly after I arrived in San Francisco, I met with David Batstone and learned about the ugly realities of human trafficking. I also learned more about poverty, hunger, and the effects of not having clean drinking water. I had been blessed beyond my wildest imagination, but the Holy Spirit was showing me that I could and should do something about the injustices and inequities experienced by a majority of the world's population. I knew I had to change. I knew I had to do *something*.

As a professional baseball player, I understand that a portion of the population looks up to me. Because I can throw a fastball at ninety-plus miles per hour, I have been given an open door to speak into the lives of younger generations. I didn't go to seminary, and I don't work in a church, but I truly believe that what I do for a living provides me a platform to share the life and love of Jesus with young people. I see myself as a youth minister. I am an advocate for the younger generation, encouraging them to use the gifts and talents God has given to them to dream big and make a difference in this world.

With the help of some friends, I started Generation Alive (GA) in 2005 as a non-profit youth ministry organization to stir a movement among the younger generations (<www.generationalive.org>). Movements begin with passion and prayer. Almost every spiritual movement throughout history started when young people prayed and took their faith seriously.

Generation Alive works in collaboration with other compassion-based organizations toward the goal of partnering with younger generations to serve those living in extreme poverty through the creative, compassionate, and redemptive love of Jesus. Generation Alive centers on four areas:

1. Ending modern-day slavery in partnership with Not for Sale.
2. Building clean water wells in partnership with Living Water International.

3. Building orphanages in partnership with the Global Orphan Project.

4. Feeding the hungry in partnership with Youthfront's Something to Eat initiative.

Too many churches and youth ministries do not give youth sufficient opportunities to serve. Tomorrow's leaders are *already* leading today. They are leading at their schools and on their sports teams. They have passion and a desire to make a difference now, not just play games and listen to sermons. Today's youth are ready to follow Jesus on a journey of love and justice, and they need the older generations to help provide opportunities, to equip them and to walk alongside them on the way. Today's youth need the space to make the decisions that *seem best* to them, learning from their mistakes along the way.

In Acts 15 the Early Church had to decide the requirements for Gentiles to be accepted in the movement. They sent their answer via a letter, which we read in verse 28: "It seemed good to the Holy Spirit and to us." This is part of what it means to live by faith, doing what "seems good" at the time and trusting the leadership and guidance of the Holy Spirit at work with you and your community.

After I started getting involved in abolition work through Not for Sale, I learned about the water crisis in Africa. Many children are missing school, some walking *seven miles* a day to get dirty water contaminated with feces, diseases, and worms just to stay alive. They drink this water and bathe in it. They cook with this water, clean dishes with it, and wash their clothes in it. They depend on this water for survival, and as cited by <www. water.org> in January 2011, it is killing them. Half of the world's hospitalizations are due to water-related diseases. Every twenty seconds a child dies from a water-related disease. Approximately one in eight people lacks access to safe drinking water. We flush our toilets every day and don't even think twice that the water in that toilet is cleaner than the drinking water in other countries. I learned about the work of Living Water International, called them, and ended up funding a clean water well project in Kazaara, Uganda.

My friends Carla and Tracey, on behalf of Generation Alive, flew to Uganda to celebrate the opening of the well. They sent me video footage of kids standing in the field under the water. It was clear water, not green or yellow or brown. The children were dancing under it, celebrating this water that is life to them.

I believe this honors the mission Jesus Christ calls us to embrace.

Jesus once said, "Let anyone who is thirsty come to me and drink. Whoever believes in me, as Scripture has said, rivers of living water will flow from within them" (John 7:37-38). When the kids were drinking this water, they were getting a taste of Jesus. Their diseases were being healed, and hope is extended because of the water. This is the kind of movement I want to help create.

When youth get the opportunity to join in with a project like this—when they see that the fruit of their labor is bringing life and joy to people they've never met—they get a taste of the joy of God's in-breaking kingdom. They are literally extending the good news of Jesus to the ends of the world. They will see that they are major contributors in the fight against poverty and other social injustices facing youth around the globe.

Doing justice is demolishing the barriers that stand between a person and Jesus—whether helping the trafficked find freedom, the thirsty receive water, or the hungry obtain food.

My friend Mike King, whom I've spoken about many times in this book, is the president and CEO of Youthfront, an amazing youth ministry organization based in Kansas City (<www.youthfront.com>). I partnered with Youthfront's Something to Eat program, sending food to Haiti after the 2010 earthquake. Something to Eat packages meals containing soy protein, vitamins, vegetables, and rice at a cost of less than a quarter per meal. A family of four can be fed for a dollar; one hundred meals can be prepared for less than the cost of filling up your car with gas. Throughout the World Series Championship season, Mike and I talked about bringing Something to Eat to Spokane to fill the food banks here with one hundred thousand meals. We planned for months. Youthfront sent a semi-truck full of the all the supplies necessary to make it happen, and our Generation Alive team worked diligently to coordinate the effort. Hundreds of young people caught the vision for providing food for those facing extreme hunger.

Walker's Furniture Autograph Session—January 21, 2011

On the day before the big event, I called teammates and friends and challenged them to help support me, Generation Alive, and Something to Eat. My agent generously sponsored four thousand meals. One child I met gave a couple of bucks. Others gave as they could, too.

My father-in-law joined the project and hosted an autograph session at his downtown furniture store. Patchin Osso and The Wingman from ESPN radio came out and did a live broadcast and interview from the store, helping to promote the event. Little kids came, and I signed baseball cards and official World Series baseballs. A few students from my old high school came, sharing basketball stories against rival teams and asking for pitching advice. Parents came, and I had the chance to share with them the passions God has placed on my heart and invited them to pack food as well.

The Service Station—January 22, 2011

The Service Station is a truly unique coffee shop, period. It is a nonprofit corporation that collaborates with businesses throughout the community and concentrates its investments in local programs. The Service Station not only serves really great coffee but also serves the youth of Spokane, providing transition homes for women and assisting organizations helping AIDS and cancer patients and their families.

But the work of The Service Station extends beyond Spokane—all the way to Ethiopia. The Service Station partnered with The Dominion Trading Company and the New Covenant Foundation to work with Ethiopian farmers, creating an environment of sustainability as the farmers share in the profits because, "It is not just fair trade but *their* trade," says Scot.

In the Rift Valley, where poverty and exploitation went hand in hand, farmers are now getting the chance to participate in the global economy. A community medical center and an orphanage for homeless boys have been built. Girls are making clothing and accessories that can be purchased at the Service Station. While we enjoy a good mocha or latte, we're helping end unjust labor practices and love our neighbors. The Service Station also has a wonderful state-of-the-art auditorium, perfect for setting up tables and packing food. With the help of the Generation Alive staff and a few Youthfront staff from Kansas City, we were ready.

Often when we think about those who are hungry, we imagine the poor in Africa, Haiti, or South America.

We have seen the pictures on television of swollen bellies and associate the poor with the label "them." But poverty is out of control in the United States as well. The following statistics were obtained in January 2011 from <www.feedingamerica.org. Over forty-six million people live in poverty in the United States, more than two million households. Of those, fifteen-and-a-half million are children. What this means is that one in six Americans does not have access to enough food. Every week, about five-and-a-half million people receive emergency food assistance. Many of the families who receive emergency food assistance report their household incomes are inadequate to cover their basic household expenses:

- Thirty-nine percent report choosing between buying food and paying rent.
- Thirty-four percent report choosing between buying food and paying medical bills.
- Thirty-five percent report choosing between buying food and paying for transportation.

At 1:00 P.M. the doors opened for registration, and the excitement was tangible. After thirty minutes, the line of those waiting to serve wrapped halfway around the outside of The Service Station. Around four hundred young people lined up to help, to serve, to volunteer their time on a Saturday afternoon to feed the hungry in Spokane. I was amazed and humbled by the attitude and passion demonstrated by the teens. With smiles on their faces and hairnets on their heads, they talked and joked and worked—pouring rice and vitamins, heat-sealing packages, taping up boxes.

Every forty-five minutes we rang a bell and invited everyone gathered into a time of silence and prayer. We wanted to acknowledge that our work was for the glory of God and to take the time to form these young people in the way of Jesus Christ. The air was pregnant with the Spirit of God. When we choose to love our neighbors as ourselves, God is uniquely present.

Jesus said that whatever we do to for "the least," we do for Him. In the course of four hours on a Saturday, soccer players, youth groups, teens from all the area schools—even a couple of four-year-olds—helped prepare seventy-five thousand meals.

They served their neighbors.

They served Jesus.

Nearly half of the world's population woke up this morning with the need for something to eat as the most pressing issue they would face this day. Consistently, Jesus has things to say about this.

In Matthew 25 Jesus speaks about some of the differences between sheep and goats (followers of Jesus and non-followers). Jesus implies that one of the things followers of Jesus do is to give food to those who are hungry. In giving something to eat to those who are hungry, we directly engage in the ministry of Jesus. "I was hungry and you gave me something to eat" (Matthew 25:35).

Another time, Jesus finds himself surrounded by a huge crowd. Jesus has compassion on the crowd because they are like sheep without a shepherd. His disciples are concerned because the crowd is hungry and there is no food with which to feed them. The disciples want Jesus to dismiss the crowd, but Jesus has other plans and instructs His disciples, "You give them something to eat" (Luke 9:13).

In the first two years of Something to Eat's existence, more than thirty thousand people (mostly teenagers) from one thousand-plus churches representing more than thirty-five states have participated in packaging more than two million meals. Those involved in providing Something to Eat meals for the hungry have been challenged to live their lives for God instead of living self-absorbed lives. Jesus asks us to give them something to eat, and young people are discovering that participating in God's agenda for restoration and redemption is the most compelling way to live.

Toward the end of his life, Paul wrote to Timothy these words:

> Command those who are rich in this present world not to be arrogant nor to put their hope in wealth, which is so uncertain, but to put their hope in God, who richly provides us with everything for

our enjoyment. Command them to do good, to be rich in good deeds, and to be generous and willing to share. In this way they will lay up treasure for themselves as a firm foundation for the coming age, so that they may take hold of the life that is truly life (*1 Timothy 6:17-19*).

In a world that teaches us to live only for self and purports that there is no greater good than money, these teens preached with their lives the radical, transforming love of God. They got a taste of life that is truly life.

These days when I play ball, I play for the other guys on my team, that they would know the joy of winning. I play for the hungry, knowing that as I get paid for exercising my gifts, I can give to help them. I play for those trapped in slavery, committed to ending the travesty of trafficking. I play for the thirsty, to help them continue developing wells in Africa and around the world. I play for the orphans and pray for a forever home for them. I play for the hungry, who need something to eat.

These days when I play ball, I play for Jesus Christ. I feel blessed to have seen my dreams of playing baseball turn into reality. I hope and pray that God will continue to birth new dreams within me that are beyond anything I can imagine.

FOURTEEN

A LOT OF PEOPLE ASK ME WHAT I'M SAYING
WHEN THEY SEE ME TALKING ON THE MOUND.
I TELL THEM I'M PRAYING. I PRAY FOR MERCY
AND WISDOM AND TRY TO DO MY BEST WITH
THE GIFTS GOD HAS ENTRUSTED TO ME.

IT WAS TIME to take my stand from sixty feet, six inches.

I played baseball with the hope of pitching in a situation just like this—the World Series, the game on the line, competing against the best hitters in the game. I fully realized that there is some portion of good luck in even getting to play in the World Series. I was teammates with Ken Griffey Jr., who played for twenty-two seasons without ever getting to the World Series. Having now played in three World Series, I consider myself blessed by God's great mercy for the opportunity.

Bochy called the bullpen with the game tied and the heart of the Detroit Tigers lineup due at the plate. In the 2010 World Series I played a key part in a game that got us into the series. This postseason, however, with our season on the line, I was pitching in all the key games. If I contributed to the loss, we would have to play another game in Detroit, and the momentum switch could increase. It was incredibly stressful and intense, but I felt God's peace surrounding me. Over the last several years God had prepared me to thrive in situations like these.

In the National League Divisional Series against the Cincinnati Reds, with the Reds up two games to none, I was brought in to pitch with the game tied. I threw two scoreless innings, and we won game three in extra innings. Our bats were hot in the fourth game, and we tied the series at two games apiece. We now had the fragile hope of sweeping Cincinnati in Cincinnati in order to move to the next round of the playoffs—something no team had been able to do to them throughout the regular season. In the fifth and final game we were leading by three runs when I entered the game. Matt Cain had pitched well, giving us the lead and a good possibility of moving to the National League Championship Series.

With two outs and two runners on, Ryan Ludwick stepped up to the plate—the potential tying run. In his previous at-bat against Cain, Ludwick had homered and cut the lead in half. After working the count full, Ryan Ludwick hit a simple grounder back to me. I was grateful, thankful to end the inning on a simple play. However, as I ran to first I felt a tweak in my knee. *Not again.*

Early in the season, after playing a day game, I went home to spend precious time with my family. Walker, my oldest son, is a big boy for his age. At the age of five, he's more than four and a half feet tall, seventy pounds, and incredibly strong. He ran to me as I knelt down to hug him, and he jumped up on my knee. Immediately I knew something wasn't right. My knee had twisted toward my other knee and I felt a pop, a bad omen for any knee. I picked up Walker, and was able to walk, but the longer I was up, the stiffer my knee became. That night I took Walker upstairs to bed and noticed that the pain in my knee was getting stronger. After a restless night, I finally decided to get out of bed at 4:00 A.M. and almost fell over because I could not move my knee. I hobbled to the kitchen and pulled out a bag of frozen vegetables and started icing the knee immediately.

The pain intensified during the couple of hours I waited to call the trainer. I could almost see him rolling his eyes over the phone as I explained to him what happened. *What other major league athlete gets injured hugging his son?* I met the trainer and had an MRI, only to discover that there was a partial tear on the attachment of my medial collateral ligament (MCL). The good news: no surgery was required for my knee to heal. The bad news: I would be placed on the DL and needed a knee brace to prevent my knee from moving in the wrong direction.

When I came off the disabled list, the knee brace I had to wear changed my pitching mechanics so that I couldn't naturally pitch the same as I had grown accustomed to pitching. Instead, the knee brace *improved* how I pitched, forcing me to land in a better position, allowing me to finish on my front side and increasing my velocity. Thanks to the knee brace, my pitches were breaking more and coming across the plate at better angles. God had once again turned my pain into something good.

Early in September in a game against the Arizona Diamondbacks, I was fielding a high chopper over my head. I snagged the ball and turned quickly to throw to first base against an extremely fast hitter—now runner. As I turned, I felt another tweak in my knee and again woke up the next day with it feeling stiff and sore. For the rest of the season, whenever I turned my foot or tried and run, my leg would not cooperate. It felt numb, weak, and unable to support me.

So when Ludwick hit the ball back to me, I was initially excited. My instinct was to run the ball toward first and flip it to Brandon Belt for the last out of the inning. I started running and felt the knee go weak. Almost falling over, I hurriedly flung the ball to Belt and tried to keep my balance. After the out was recorded, I continued running past first with serious pain. I hobbled into the dugout and said that something had happened to my knee. Pitching coach Dave Righetti wanted to keep me in the game to face the first hitter in the eighth, lefty Jay Bruce.

I hurried to the locker room to work with the trainers. They applied heat to my knee and encouraged me to walk around in in order to keep my knee warm. I tried to pay attention to what was happening in the game, knowing that continuing our season was still not a sure thing. I walked up the stairs to ask the trainer how many outs there were. At the precise moment I reached the top stair, Gregor Blanco took a check swing and lined the ball straight for the dugout. Righetti, who was partially protecting me, ducked out of the way. The ball was coming straight at my forehead. Without thinking, I spun away from the ball and jumped back—still on the stairs—and landed with all my weight on the thumb of my pitching hand. It is almost impossible to throw a ball without a strong, healthy thumb.

At first, the pain was so intense I thought my thumb was broken. I went straight to the X-ray room at the stadium and was thankful to learn it wasn't broken. However, the ligament was severely sprained. Eventually we did win the game, and I celebrated our victory on the field with a sore knee as well as a brace on my left hand.

The following day was an off day, and the team remained in Cincinnati to see if we would be playing the St. Louis Cardinals or the Washington Nationals. I tried to play catch, but my thumb hurt so badly I couldn't throw the ball with any power or accuracy. I started worrying and praying as the trainers continued to work on my thumb and my knee.

Only three days after landing on my thumb, I was back on the mound, facing the St. Louis Cardinals and former teammate Carlos Beltran. One of my strikeout pitches, one of the pitches hitters know I have, is a sweeping curveball. However, my thumb hurt so much there was no way I could throw the curveball. In fact, throughout the entire series against the Cardinals, I threw only three or four curveballs, and only one of those was a strike. Oddly enough, because I was pitching hurt and because I was focused on my thumb, my pitches were actually better. I wasn't overthrowing or trying to do too much but was trying to keep everything simple. Again,

God in His great mercy was faithful to use me in spite of my weakness and pain.

I pitched pretty well in three of the first four games against the Cardinals, but as a team we were down three games to one. Our season was again on the line. In game five Barry Zito shut down and shut out the Cardinals; we closed the series to within a game. Momentum started to swing back our way.

In game six we scored five runs early, and I pitched to three hitters in the eighth inning. Even though my thumb still hurt, I was feeling good about the results, and the team was playing well. We tied the series against the Cardinals and were only one game away from returning to the World Series for the second time in three years.

In the decisive seventh game our pitching again shut out the Cardinals, and we won 9 to 0. For the final three games we had outscored the Cardinals 20 to 1. Our offense was clicking on all cylinders as we prepared to face one of the most explosive offenses in all of baseball—the Detroit Tigers.

In the World Series our offense continued to put up runs and our pitching continued to dominate hitters. We won game 1 of the World Series 8 to 3 and then shut out the Tigers to win the next two games by the same score, 2 to 0. In a series where most thought we were the slight underdog, we were now leading three games to none, one win away from another championship.

Matt Cain pitched a brilliant game four, leaving with the game tied at three after seven innings. I had already warmed up an inning earlier when the call came that I would be pitching the eighth inning. In my quick bullpen session, I threw the best pitches I had thrown all season. There is always the fear that what happens in the bullpen won't translate to the field, but I was ready and confident. I knew I was doing exactly what God had called me to do. I continued praying as I pitched and was truly excited to take the field and be part of the game.

I wasn't the same as a pitcher or person this post-season as I had been in the 2010 World Series. God had led me on a journey to places I couldn't begin to imagine, opening my eyes to worldwide injustices and impressing upon me my responsibility to speak up, to take action, to "do justice" and "love my neighbor as myself." I recognized that God has placed me in a role of leadership and given me a platform of influence. There is always the temptation to use this platform for selfish ends or purposes. As a Christ follower and someone whose heart's desire is to live out the love and glory of God, I pray constantly that God will use my abilities and actions so that others might know the love of Jesus.

I knew that I would be facing the heart of the Tiger line-up in pinch-hitter Avisail Garcia, followed by Triple Crown winner Miguel Cabrera and Prince Fielder. If anyone got on base, Delmon Young was the fourth hitter. The bullpen gate opened, and as soon as my foot hit the warning track, I heard the whisper of God: *Tonight, I will expand your platform.* I almost started crying. I knew that I was on holy ground and that I was in a sacred place. I was almost overwhelmed by the tangible presence of God's Spirit. I felt strong and at peace on the mound, as if I were pitching for the greatness and glory of God alone.

A lot of people ask me what I'm saying when they see me talking on the mound. I tell them I'm praying. I pray for mercy and wisdom and try to do my best with the gifts God has entrusted to me.

Avisail Garcia worked the count full, and I ended up walking him. I remember saying, *God, this isn't what I was thinking you meant by expanding my platform.* The winning run was now on base, and Detroit's three biggest bats were stepping up to the plate.

Miguel Cabrera was the first person to win the Triple Crown in forty-five years, leading the American League with a .330 batting average, 44 home runs, and 139 RBIs. He was also the first hitter I had to face with a runner on base. Even with Cabrera at the plate—even with my thumb throbbing—I felt my pitches were continuing to get better. I kept praying for God's mercy and grace, for His wisdom from pitch to pitch. I was finally in the place that, even if Cabrera hit it out of the park, I still knew that God is all good. When Cabrera struck out swinging at a split-finger fastball, I felt the echo of the Spirit: *Tonight, I am expanding your platform.*

Over the last six years I have faced Prince Fielder a dozen times when he played for the Milwaukee Brewers. He was hitting .333 against me, 4-for-12, and had seen everything I can throw. The first pitch was a ball, followed by a called strike. Even though my thumb continued to hurt, I decided to throw a curveball, throwing what might have been the best curveball of my career. Fielder was so fooled by the curve he flinched as the pitch dropped in for strike two. To be completely honest, even I thought the pitch was going to hit him when I released it. Fielder then swung and missed at a sinker inside for the second out and my second strikeout.

Delmon Young was next. Young had homered against Cain in the bottom of the sixth inning to tie the game at 3. I continued praying and remained focused. I pitched Young almost exactly as I pitched Cabrera and ended up striking him out on another split-finger fastball.

I was pumped as I walked off the field. However, Andy Dirks was on deck, and since he is a left-handed hitter, I knew I was still in the game. My thumb was getting stiff in the cold Detroit evening. I sat next to the heater and kept a heat pack on my thumb, hoping to get a few more quality pitches out of it. Without my thumb I couldn't throw curveballs.

I returned to the mound in the bottom of the ninth inning; game four of the World Series. This is the dream of kids around the world. Dirks fouled off a couple of good pitches, and then I struck him out, making it four consecutive strikeouts.

I stayed in the game to face right-handed hitting shortstop Johnny Peralta. Peralta drilled a 2-0 pitch to center, and with the way the wind was blowing out, I cringed and expected the worse. *As good as I've pitched, please, this can't be how it ends tonight.* Angel Pagan ran back to the fence, and then I felt the wind shift. Pagan came in a few steps toward left field and made the catch. I could breathe again and continued praying. Santiago Casilla came in to get the final out of the ninth. The game would go to extra innings.

I talked to Pagan after the inning, and he said, "I couldn't believe that ball was going out, but the wind seemed to keep pushing it. Then, it was like the wind blew the ball the opposite way and knocked it down, and I almost dropped it." We laughed together, and I thanked him for saving me and making the play.

In the top of the tenth inning, with two outs, Marco Scutaro singled to center field to score Ryan Theriot. Sergio Romo closed out the game by striking out the side in the bottom of the tenth to give the San Francisco Giants their second World Championship in three years. And on a cold, crisp, October night, we were oblivious to the weather as we celebrated the pinnacle of baseball achievements—another World Series ring.

Not only did I get a lot of post-season attention for pitching ten innings with ten strikeouts and no earned runs, but my beautiful wife, Larisa, received quite a bit of media attention. Our first son, Walker, was born in August 2007, and I went to the World Series with the Colorado Rockies after an amazing win streak to get us there. Our second son, Logan, was born in September 2010, and we ended up winning the World Series with the Giants. Our third son, Kolt, was born in August 2012, and we won the World Series again. This story was picked up by news and sports media across the country. We had a lot of fun with it. Along with getting a new three-year contract to continue playing for the San Francisco Giants, I tried to get a deal done between the Giants and Larisa for a birth incentive clause. I think the Giants might have gone for it, but I'm not sure Larisa's up for it.

God has been faithful and has extended the platform He has given me, fulfilling the words the Spirit whispered to me as I stepped out on the warning track. Generation Alive in Spokane has partnered with churches, schools— even baseball teams—to package meals through the Something to Eat program, feeding tens of thousands of our neighbors who are hungry. I love living in Spokane, where I grew up, met my wife, and began the process of raising our family. I also love that we get to be so involved in the life of San Francisco, working with Not for Sale to eliminate sex trafficking around the world. I love that in San Francisco, through Generation Alive and Youthfront's Something to Eat initiative, urban public school kids have packed nearly a quarter of a million meals for people living in the famine zone caused by drought and civil conflict in the Horn of Africa and for children living in the orphanages of earthquake-damaged Haiti.

I recently hung out for an entire day with four hundred fifty high school students in East Palo Alto to package one hundred thousand meals for our Something to Eat initiative. East Palo Alto is a suburb of San Francisco and is divided from Palo Alto by a freeway. Palo Alto is a very wealthy area fueled by the success of the Silicon Valley. Apple, Google, and Facebook are some of the corporations connected to Palo Alto. East Palo Alto lies in stark contrast. About sixty-five percent of the residents of East Palo Alto are Hispanic/Latino, sixteen percent are African-American, and ten percent are Pacific Islander/ Asian. Several years ago Michelle Pfeiffer starred in the movie *Dangerous Minds,* in which she played a teacher who taught at an East Palo Alto high school. In the movie the students' lives were being destroyed by drugs, gang involvement, illicit sex, and crime. Living in East Palo Alto is still a dangerous reality for a young person. In the few months before our Something to Eat event, several young people were killed through drug and gang violence. However, on this day something truly unique happened. Many young people were being called out of the lives that they were trapped in—drugs, crime, gangs, violence—and suddenly finding themselves in a story of restoration and hope. They even raised money to provide food for those who were less fortunate than they. We worked hard all day, yet these teenagers didn't want to take a break. We stopped for short five-minute breaks throughout the event to talk about and reflect on why we were doing what we were doing, exchange information about the world hunger crises, discuss the importance of taking care of each other, and share inspirational thoughts. Local artists performed street poetry that was uplifting and spiritually rich. It was amazing to see what was unfolding. The East Palo Alto Police Captain spent the day with us. He was so enthusiastic about what was happening that he was on the phone talking to the news media, reminding them that they were all at the recent murder scenes involving young people, and they needed to come see the good things young people were doing. Many of these young people found themselves caught up in participation of God's movement of restoration and hope for the first time in their lives.

We're dreaming now of hosting an event to package one million meals, to show teens and others that loving their neighbors and making a difference is an important part of God allowing us to participate in His movement toward restoration.

This book began with the story of me almost becoming a victim of human trafficking when I was a child in Thailand. I am preparing to return there for the first time since childhood. Thailand is one of the darkest places for human trafficking, a place where I could have lost my life if I had been trafficked as a young boy. I know this trip will have a transformational impact on my life and deepen my resolve to do all I can to end the travesty of sex trafficking.

I'll see through a new lens of awareness and compassion those who have been trafficked and exploited. I'll remember and reflect upon the time that I was nearly dragged into the ugly reality of child sex trafficking. I will use the platform that God has given me to declare the greatness of God's justice around the world. I so long for the day when God's kingdom fully breaks into the present from God's future and God gets His way on earth as in heaven

God has faithfully walked with me on a serendipitous and providential journey, teaching me how to pray, how to forgive, how to serve, how to trust His way when it seems the world around me is falling apart, and most of all, how to love my neighbor as myself.

In this crazy world in which we live a guy who can throw a baseball ninety miles an hour can make millions of dollars and indulge in every whim and desire, flaunting his gifts and taking his talent for granted.

God freely gives gifts so that we might learn to give generously and gratefully to those in need around us. When I step up on the mound, I pray to be faithful, to remember who I am and to whom I belong. There will be times on the field when I succeed beyond my wildest dreams—and times when I turn and watch the ball fly to the other side of the fence. In both of these circumstances the Holy Spirit is unveiling the story of God's coming kingdom through this pitcher. I will strive to live faithfully in the way of Jesus and do all I can to stir a movement that declares the goodness of God, is shaped by the ministry of the Holy Spirit, and seeks to bear witness to the restorative work of Jesus Christ for the joy of the whole world.

AFTERWORD

GOD is a God of ridiculous grace. I spend eight to nine months a year with world-class athletes. Some of them believe in Jesus, some of them believe in self, and some of them pretend that it's not important to believe in anything. Some of the stuff I hear preached from pulpits works only if you lock yourself in a Christian subculture that looks nothing similar to the Kingdom that Jesus proclaimed and lived. If I lived in the black-and-white world that is so often preached about, I would completely alienate myself from my teammates.

Jesus told us to love God and love our neighbor. It's not easy to love your neighbor as yourself. Do you like the taste of an ice-cold cup of water? Do you think your neighbor should have the same privilege? Do you like to eat? If so, how do you walk past the hungry and do nothing?

We are called to live out the love of Jesus—to love mercy, work for justice, to humble ourselves, and to serve others. We should pray wherever we are, continuing the conversation that God started when we were called into marvelous light. We must refuse to condemn, for we have not walked in others' shoes. Let's choose to believe that love will once again stir a movement among us that will be fully cooperative with God's mission to make all things new, longing for a day when all people will know the greatness and goodness of the King.

Until that day when I see my Lord Jesus Christ face to face, whether I'm pitching or sitting on the bench or even playing ball at all, I will steadfastly seek the face of the Savior, who loved me and gave himself for me.

EXTRA INNINGS: ONE FINAL STORY

THE SAN FRANCISCO GIANTS have an amazing and storied baseball legacy. I've met and spent time with Willie Mays and Willie McCovey, with Gaylord Perry and Will Clark, and numerous others. You never know who will be in the clubhouse on any given day.

One day shortly after I arrived in San Francisco, I saw Barry Bonds sitting in the manager's office. Everyone in the clubhouse knows that Barry is one of those guys with a dry sense of humor, so I decided to test it out.

I walked into the office, extended my hand, and said, "Hey, I'm Jeremy Affeldt." He reached out and shook my hand. I looked back at him and said, "You?" He glanced around the office. I said, "Yeah, I introduced myself and didn't catch your name." Barry couldn't believe what I said. I could read the expression on his face: *Is this guy serious?*

"Barry," I said breaking the silence, "I know who you are."

He looked at me and flashed a million-dollar smile, "I like you, kid." It was quite funny.

Sometimes we choose to live in such small and serious circles we forget that God is smiling, delighting in His children and whispering, "I like you, kid."